The Heart
of the
Matter

Other Lake Hickory Resources

George W. Bullard Jr., Senior Editor
GBullard@TheColumbiaPartnership.org

Christ-Centered Coaching
7 Benefits for Ministry Leaders
by Jane Creswell

From the Outside in
Connecting to the Community around You
by Ronald W. Johnson

Operation Inasmuch
Mobilizing Believers beyond the Walls of the Church
by David W. Crocker

Pursuing the Full Kingdom Potential of Your Congregation
by George W. Bullard Jr.

Seeds for the Future
Growing Organic Leaders for Living Churches
by Robert D. Dale

Spiritual Leadership in a Secular Age
Building Bridges Instead of Barriers
by Edward H. Hammett

Other Leadership Resources

Courageous Church Leadership
Conversations with Effective Practitioners
by John Chandler

Recreating the Church
Leadership for the Postmodern Age
by Richard L. Hamm

www.lakehickoryresources.com

The Heart of the Matter

Changing the World God's Way

CHARLES HALLEY

Lake Hickory RESOURCES

Cover and interior design: Elizabeth Wright

Visit www.lakehickoryresources.com

10 9 8 7 6 5 4 3 2 1   06 07 08 09 10 11

Library of Congress Cataloging–in–Publication Data

Halley, Charles.
    Heart of the matter : changing the world God's way / Charles Halley.
        p. cm.
    Includes bibliographical references.
    ISBN-13: 978-0-8272-1452-1 (pbk. : alk. paper)
    ISBN-10: 0-8272-1452-9 (pbk. : alk. paper)
    1. Christian life. 2. Church. I. Title.
    BV4501.3.H3485 2006
    253–dc22

                                                    2006006315

Printed in the United States of America

Ongoing
To Mary Lou—my earthly partner—whose ongoing
love and support has encouraged me
to keep taking new steps of faith.

Relative
To my mentors—especially Bob Tuttle—who have
helped me understand God in the context
of my own life experience.

Purposeful
To the lay leaders of Christ's Church
for whom this book has been written.

Contentious
To my many friends in Christ who have
sharpened me by their honesty and love.

Cooperative
To my heavenly Partners—Three in One—whose
patience and compassion defy reason or logic.

Contents

Editor's Foreword

Inspiration and Wisdom for
Twenty-first–Century Christian Leaders

You have chosen wisely in deciding to study and learn from a **Lake Hickory Resources** book. Lake Hickory Resources publishes for the following:

- congregational leaders who desire to serve effectively
- Christian ministers who pursue excellence in service
- congregations that desire to reach their full Kingdom potential
- denominational and parachurch leaders who want to come alongside affiliated congregations in a servant leadership role

Lake Hickory Resources began as an inspiration- and wisdom-sharing vehicle of Lake Hickory Learning Communities. LHLC is the web of relationships developing from the base of Hollifield Leadership Center (www.Hollifeld.org) near Hickory, North Carolina. As of September 2006, Lake Hickory Resources has become a publishing venture of The Columbia Partnership, found at www.TheColumbiaPartnership.org.

The mission of **Lake Hickory Resources** currently is being expressed through two meaningful avenues. First, George Bullard, Strategic Coordinator for The Columbia Partnership, also is senior editor for *Net Results* magazine (www.NetResults.org), a national, transdenominational publication that appears monthly in print or electronic form.

Second, **Lake Hickory Resources** publishes books in partnership with Christian Board of Publication. Once this partnership is in full production, it will produce eight to twelve new books each year.

We welcome your comments on these books, and we welcome your suggestions for new subject areas and authors we ought to consider.

George W. Bullard Jr., Senior Editor
GBullard@TheColumbiaPartnership.org

Foreword

True spirituality is a community affair. Increasingly, the staunch individualism of the Western Church has gotten her deeper and deeper into trouble. Perhaps the old spiritual, "Oh that will be glory for me, glory for me, glory for me," needs another chorus. Church is not a cacophony of individuals; she is her several parts baptized by one Spirit into one body—a community. We evangelicals have an expression: "God has no grandchildren, only children." While that may be true, most of God's children are born into communities that wield powerful influences on their children's lifelong decisions. Most of the world thinks and acts not only in extended families, but as whole communities. African wisdom insists, "It takes an entire village to raise a child." What is sometimes omitted is that this has reciprocity. African author Alexander McCall Smith states it well: "In return that child would in due course feel responsible for everyone in that village.[1] In his poem, "The Rainbow," Wordsworth gives a slightly different perspective,

> The Child is father of the Man;
> I could wish my days to be
> *Bound each to each* by natural piety.[2]

Charles Halley has taken the important concepts of what it means to be godly as an individual and applied them to the church as a whole. Just as most of the world sees Westerners as lacking humility and global perspective, Halley sees much of the Church as all too often bent on its own needs, oblivious to the world around it, and oblivious to what it means to be a community of believers that ministers out of a community ethos. All of that is to say that throughout this book you will find a healthy balance between individual disciple and community discipleship.

The heart of the problem seems to be our inability to translate what works for a few individuals into a process of spirituality that identifies the church as a whole. Can a church have a few healthy body parts but be sick unto death? Can it be less than the sum of its parts? Halley thinks that it can if it does not understand the concepts of congregational disciplines. Happily, those are given to us here in some detail.

A reoccurring theme develops early. The church must exchange the kind of a world in which it is at the center for the kind of a world in which God is at the center. I was fortunate enough to see my daughter being born. When she took her first breath, I wept for joy. As I looked at her, I remember thinking, "She's so perfect we won't have to get her baptized." That impression lasted only a few minutes. Within seconds she was screaming as if the entire universe revolved around her mouth, "Feed me! Now!" Psychologists have a name for that—Narcissism. Bonhoeffer wrote, "Life was intended to be lived *from* the Center, not *at* the center." Halley is right. We mature as Christians—and as churches—when we make the kinds of decisions that enable us to exchange the kind of reality in which *we* are at the center for the kind of reality in which *God* is at the center.

On a more personal note, I have known Charles Halley for nearly thirty years. Although I knew him first as a student, he is now a trusted colleague and friend. I trust his judgment. I always profit from his insights. I like his book. It is thoroughly readable, practical, applicable, and workable. I pray that you will give it a serious read, take its teaching to heart, experience the church as God intended for it to be, and then change the world. Let God arise!

Robert Tuttle Jr.

Acknowledgments

Think of me as a Christian pearl collector who decided it was time to strand some in book form. Truth be told, I have been picking them up for over thirty years—blessed by numerous faithful disciples from coast to coast.

In my youth, I picked up a bunch of pearls in Texas and am grateful to those who saw more in me than I saw in myself. Among the many who fall into this category, I would identify Bill Edwards, Tom Tyndall, Jim Smith, and Mike Beidel as special mentors.

When I left Fuller Theological Seminary, I had gathered a lot more pearls—some of which I am still polishing. I was mightily blessed by the godly wisdom of fellow students like Stan Slade and Bill Edwards, and to beloved mentors like Bob Tuttle Jr. I would also highlight Dan Fuller, Bill Pannell, Robert Munger, and Roberta Hestenes among the many others who made a profound difference.

In Michigan—akin to everywhere I have ever lived—I found strong disciples willing to share their treasures. God regularly used people such as Tom and Judy Skaff, along with Dave Smith, to teach me new and important lessons. Even those I sought to minister to—especially the youth leaders—became instruments that shaped my understanding of Christ's church.

In North Carolina, I have been showered with even more pearls and am grateful to Bob Walkup and David Brownlee for their support as I partnered with them in two different congregations. Each has inspired me to take the risk of stranding the accumulating pearls into my own book. I am also grateful to the many disciples within these two congregations and especially my current staff partners at Covenant Church. All have taught me much about kingdom values and priorities.

This book's bibliography is full of other disciples—many of whom I have never met—whose insights have significantly contributed to my maturation as a Christian thinker. Of particular benefit have been the writings of Richard Foster, Bill Easum, and Tom Bandy. Having now completed my first book, I more fully appreciate their hard work in communicating their own wonderful pearls for the sake of Christ's church. And I would be remiss if I did not also mention Don Cousins. Don's teachings have greatly influenced me in recent years as I have sought to understand the biblical notion of equipping.

In regards to this book, I am most indebted to my editorial partner, Barb Sibley. Without her, it simply would not have happened–period. Though I might take some credit for stranding the pearls, she polished them beyond my expectations.

Obviously, I will be forever grateful to my wife, Mary Lou, who has willingly and enthusiastically encouraged me to follow my dreams for twenty-nine years and loved me consistently and well, even when I made U-turns! She, as well as my three boys, has been an inspiration through it all.

And finally, I acknowledge the source of all the pearls–my Creator. In reality, neither the pearls nor the strand is mine–I'm just the messenger. Thanks be to God!

Introduction

*For the eyes of the L*ORD *range throughout the earth to strengthen those whose hearts are fully committed to him.*

2 CHRONICLES 16:9

My good friend Tom was at the end of his rope. He had tried almost everything to light a fire under his congregation. After seven challenging years, he found himself tired, discouraged, and sure of only one thing–his job security was hanging by a thread.

Before he arrived, Tom had met with the church leaders and gotten the lay of the land. At that time, he was convinced the congregation was ripe for a genuine overhaul: he envisioned leading his flock to a renewed commitment to God and a genuine enthusiasm for the Great Commission–going and making disciples everywhere (Mt. 28:18–20). In short order, though, he saw that the mindset of the majority was intent upon maintaining the status quo and caring for those safely within the walls of the church.

Tom, ever the optimist, was not deterred. With patience and an eagerness to learn, he began to hunt for the keys to cultivating a faithful church. One question brought focus to his search: *What could he do to promote and foster a change in the church's values and priorities–its culture–so that the members would willingly stop "doing" church and start "being" a church that took seriously the biblical call to make disciples of all nations?*

Tom left no stone unturned in his single-minded pursuit to find the best strategies and programs to spur faithfulness among his church's people. He prayed fervently, read scores of relevant books, and sought out dozens of seasoned Christian leaders. With teams of laity, he attended conferences to glean the best practices designed to heighten a church's spiritual health and vibrancy. He deliberately zeroed in on his church leaders, seeking to inspire in them a sense of urgency for ministry to the surrounding community.

Tom paved the way for small group ministry. He worked with a team to overhaul his church's worship style, seeking to make it inviting to the unchurched. He championed a spiritual gifts ministry that empowered laypeople to use the spiritual talents God gave them. Tom invested himself in training ministry leaders so that they, in turn, could train others. Finally, Tom made sure that the nurture that members received from Bible study also equipped them to share the gospel with those who were hurting and lost.

So, what was the combined result of his dedication and energy? As you might have guessed from the opening, a congregation that remained mired in its past, and a deeply troubled pastor.

My Parallel Journey

During the same seven years, I was on staff at a nearby church. My church community was vibrant, innovative, and rapidly growing. Nonetheless, I was grappling with the same types of questions that Tom was seeking to answer:

> How can today's churches sustain the same transforming power of the Holy Spirit that was clearly evident in the earliest Christian congregations? In other words, what fuels the movement of the Holy Spirit among God's gathered people? Why are some churches on fire while others are stone cold? And what—if anything—can faithful leaders do to turn their dying or stagnant churches around?

Why bother with these issues? Didn't my church have a lock on the right "formula"? Actually, the challenge I saw was not so much to light a congregational fire but to keep the flame burning. I wanted to avoid the complacency that usually comes with success.

What I Learned along the Way

Fortunately, I found and gleaned a wealth of wisdom from many excellent Christian resources focusing on congregational transformation and vitality.[1] I also benefited from delving into the recent writings of behavioral science, particularly the study of organizational development—*the planned process of change within an organization's culture.*[2] Having been an instructor at a nearby college, I had taught organizational behavior, making me even more aware of the human dynamics of the church. Finally, my unusual combination of work experiences—serving as president of a multi-million-dollar business as well as pastoring within several large churches—has shown me the value of integrating the truths of social science and God's Word.

So…what did I learn along the way? First, I learned that the laity must be empowered to do ministry if a dynamic system like the church wants to be effective in a rapidly changing world. Second, I observed that teamwork is a key value and critically important to success—no surprise there! Third, I have become convinced that churches need to adapt if they are to communicate their core beliefs in relevant ways for new generations of members. Finally, I have come to appreciate the need for organizational leaders—church leaders included—to be highly intentional and focused in how they form a collective identity and establish a clear direction.

Even after gathering all these pearls of wisdom and experience, though, my basic questions remained unanswered. I clearly saw that the key to congregational transformation and vitality was *not* found in implementing ministry programs or in mastering behavioral theory. I felt compelled to dig deeper and find a biblical model that adequately explains the transformational work of the Holy Spirit in the local church. My quest has led me to craft my own convictions about the most basic starting point of spiritual transformation within the church.

The Power of a Metaphor

My search began twenty years ago when I first picked up Richard Foster's *Celebration of Discipline*.[3] The opening chapter of his great book clicked on the lights for me—an "Aha!" experience—and planted the seeds that have since germinated to become my understanding of God's work in our lives through the Holy Spirit. I was somewhat familiar with "spiritual disciplines." Foster's words, combined with my readiness to soak in their meaning, dramatically fueled my understanding of spiritual transformation and the vital role that the disciplines play in this process.

Using a great analogy, Foster describes the farmer who tills, sows, waters, and weeds to cultivate and promote a bountiful crop. Although the farmer's efforts make a real difference, ultimately God grows the plants. The farmer's discipline, though important and critical, is secondary to the renewing work of the Creator. Foster suggests that disciplines such as study, prayer, worship, fellowship, serving, and generosity do not directly cause the believer to grow spiritually; but they create an environment in which God's powerful Spirit can effectively work in ready, receptive lives.

Practicing these "spiritual habits"—and Foster describes twelve in depth—keeps our hearts open to what God is seeking to accomplish in and through us. Thus, personal spiritual transformation—the essence of discipleship—is a process, combining the life-changing work of the Spirit and the ongoing faithfulness of disciples. What a difference this helpful analogy has made in my understanding!

Several years ago, I was trying to explain the Church and the nature of congregational renewal and faithfulness to a group from a nearby church. I was struggling to find the right analogy when another light bulb went on. A crystal-clear image flashed in my brain—my own walk of faith, namely discipleship. The Church is like me! Or am I like the Church? If spiritual disciplines plainly exist that help me grow in my own faithfulness, why wouldn't disciplines for our communal growth as a church body also exist? At this point I realized that the dynamics and dimensions of church transformation draw a close parallel to personal discipleship.

Since that day, I have been exploring this concept of "congregational discipleship" through study, reflection, teaching, and dialogue. The more I focus on this area of study, the more convinced I become that the Scriptures teach both types of discipleship—personal and corporate. Both are equally relevant for the Body of Christ in today's world. Am I still learning about this subject? I always will be. As I go along, I look forward to receiving insightful feedback from you readers.

A New Paradigm for Church Renewal

Tom and I, through different paths, have arrived at the same conclusion: the absolute, nonnegotiable starting point for ongoing congregational transformation and vitality is when a church collectively responds in an authentically heartfelt way to Jesus' invitation to deny itself and follow Him. Inevitably, a genuine change of congregational values and priorities occurs: the people of God learn to exchange a self-centered world for one in which Christ and kingdom values are prioritized. This gradual process of transformation within the very heart of the church is what I call *congregational discipleship.* This transforming experience closely parallels our own journey of faith.

Congregational vitality is not about getting people to show up; it is insuring that God shows up. Growing a church numerically is relatively easy: secure an excellent communicator; add sacred music that is attractive to the intended audience, and sprinkle in relevant children's and student ministry. In due time, a crowd will arrive! Insuring that God shows up is a completely different issue. Only one highly challenging pathway exists, namely *obedience.* By obedience, I mean letting go of our personal preferences and embracing a commitment to Christ's missional agenda. When we do so, we invite God to take over and reign among us. The heart of the matter is simply this: programs attract people, but obedience attracts God. If God shows up in your church, expect His friends!

Don't misunderstand me. I am not at all discounting the value of knowing and implementing change management principles in the church, or the worth of understanding behavioral science truths. The contributions of multiple authors in these areas are significant. Nor do I discount the value of undertaking ministry programs that may provide practical help for disciples. Each of these strategies, however, is secondary when it comes to initiating and sustaining a spiritual transformation process within a church.

The bottom line of congregational discipleship lies in one crucial issue. Any church that yearns to experience the transforming power of the Holy Spirit must continually ask itself a profoundly simple question: *Is Jesus indeed Lord and Head of the church, or are the members?* When Jesus is increasingly the center of the church—when Jesus is rightly sitting on the throne in the eyes and hearts of a congregation—the movement of the Spirit is strong, the power of sinful addictions are broken over time, and God's grace is evident to all. At that point, no church leaders, pastors, or laity will have to wonder what to "do" to be a faithful church. Spirit-supplied vitality will ooze out of the pores of that community of disciples.

Discipleship has two distinct facets, combining both what *I* do and what *we* do collectively. Discipleship is personal—focusing on transforming *me* into a faithful follower of Christ—and congregational—focusing on transforming *us*. Are these two types of discipleship related? Yes, and if you understand one, the other is much easier to grasp.

A Quick Overview

The easiest way for me to provide a quick and effective overview of this book is to discuss its three main sections using a "3-D" approach. Those three "d's"—*discipleship, dimensions, and disciplines*—are the key concepts that we will explore and grasp together. So here goes:

Part 1: Chapters 1 and 2 are a quick review of the basics of spiritual transformation and how it relates to faithful *discipleship.* Chapter 1 begins with a visual model that many of my students have found helpful, along with a distinctive definition of discipleship that will serve as a common thread throughout the text. Chapter 2 reveals how this two–step paradigm of transformation is visible throughout the pages of Scripture as well as our surrounding world. Together, these chapters provide a quick review of common knowledge—the nature of our own discipleship—which will in turn become the foundation for grasping a concept rarely articulated or understood: the spiritual dynamics of congregational transformation.

Part 2: Chapters 3 through 7 outline the five *dimensions* of congregational discipleship. Chapter 3 underscores that personal discipleship is *ongoing*—it is neither a dated event nor a one-time experience. It is a never-ending process of transformation that calls us, on a daily basis, to die to self and live for God. For the Church, discipleship is no different. Faithfulness together can never be construed as merely an event or an experience. If so, the apostles would have had every right to sit on their laurels after Pentecost, the kingpin of mountaintop experiences for Christ's Church.

Complacency never entered the apostles' minds. They knew the arrival of the Spirit was only the beginning, not the end. The Church is called to be in process—taking next steps of faith—in an ever-changing world.

Chapter 4 establishes that discipleship is also a unique process that is *relative* to where you have been, who you are, and where you are called to go. Never a series of predetermined and sequential steps or a straight path with a common starting point for all believers, discipleship is a jagged and twisted road with multiple dead-end loops. Your own journey is as unique as your thumbprint. Churches, like individual disciples, are also called to honor God based on who they are and where they are placed to serve. Congregations are well advised to compare their faithfulness to their own history and to biblical mandates rather than compare themselves to other churches.

Chapter 5 confirms that discipleship is *purposeful* and has clear objectives—we are called both to *be* and *do*. First, we are called to love the Lord with all our heart, mind, soul, and strength: this is *being*. Simultaneously, we are to love our neighbors as ourselves and use our giftedness to make disciples: this is *doing*. The purpose of the Church is different, but related to, my own call to *be* and *do*. Paul has a three-pronged strategy for creating faithful churches—invite...grow...send. Paul began new churches by (1) proclaiming the Good News and *inviting* his audience to respond, (2) *growing* responsive followers as capable servants and (3) empowering these believers by *sending* them to be ambassadors for Christ within the context of their spiritual gifts, passions, and spheres of influence. Invite...grow...send is nothing more than a process to help individual disciples be and do.

Chapter 6 details the *contentious* nature of discipleship—the inherent conflict between two kingdoms and their opposing values. We are called to live in one world and be of another. Predictably, strife surrounds us. If our own experience of faith is a struggle, why should the larger Body of Christ be any different? To make matters worse, church conflicts are very visible, not merely an internal stew of tension simmering just inside our souls. If you have ever refereed a discussion between church members with differing mindsets—those who prioritize caring for existing church members vs. those who prioritize reaching the lost (just an example, mind you!)—you know what I am talking about! Each group naturally competes for the supremacy of its particular values.

Chapter 7 concludes this section by outlining the *cooperative* dimension of discipleship. In other words, personal faithfulness occurs when God's transformational power is combined with our human discipline and the time-tested habits such as prayer, study, worship, fellowship, generosity, and service. As a result, spiritual vitality is neither a function of our own hard work nor the dominating influence of God. It is somewhere in between, a cooperative process. I will suggest that spiritual disciplines also exist for the local church—"congregational disciplines"—formative activities that foster spiritual faithfulness. I subdivide the congregational "spiritual habits" into three categories: (1) *cornerstone disciplines* that help to secure Jesus' place as the Head of the church; (2) *ministry disciplines* that help to establish His methods as the process for disciple-making; and 3) *support disciplines* that help to supply the essential resources that equipped servants need.

Part 3: The book's last section greatly expands upon these three categories of *congregational disciplines.* Chapter 8 details the three *cornerstone disciplines.* Together, they help to secure Christ's authority as Head of the church and affirm His universal mandate to make disciples. These disciplines also enable the church to claim its unique, God-inspired vision. Specifically, this section explains how, when properly exercised, the cornerstone disciplines work:

- *Cornerstone discernment* is a powerful means to encourage a church's core disciples to exchange a member-centered definition of congregational life for a Christ–centered paradigm grounded in the Great Commission. When the church's core disciples define its cornerstone—as expressed through values, beliefs, vision, and mission—the stage is set for building His kingdom, fostering humble servants, and releasing the power of God's Spirit.
- *Leadership alignment* is a powerful means to encourage a church's core disciples to exchange their cultural-based methods of governance for a biblically based community that prioritizes Jesus' disciple-making methods as defined by a shared cornerstone. When a church's leadership is united and aligned to common kingdom principles, the Spirit is given permission to accomplish more than humans can imagine.
- *Vision casting* is a powerful means to encourage the entire church to exchange its comfortable and self-fulfilling expectations for a lifestyle characterized by an urgent passion for the hurting and lost. If we love Christ, we collectively follow His Great Commission, disciple-making path; and the Spirit empowers our every step of faith.

Chapter 9 details the three *ministry disciplines.* Together, they help to establish Jesus' disciple-making strategy as the norm for all ministries in concert with the church's God-centered cornerstone. Specifically, this section explains how, when properly exercised, the ministry disciplines work:

- *Relevant worship* is a powerful means to encourage a church to exchange its preoccupation with traditional forms for an approach that effectively communicates a timeless Gospel to those in and beyond its walls. The resulting environment sets the stage for the movement of God's Spirit that can be felt and sensed by the invited guests of regular participants. And it leaves them hungry for more.

• *Spiritual formation* is a powerful means to encourage a church to exchange its own notions of truth for a world in which the God-inspired Scriptures are the manual for daily living. As the church collectively complies with the commands of Christ, God honors this faithful obedience by sending the Spirit to be present, show the way, and empower the journey.

• *Lay mobilization* is a powerful means to encourage a church to exchange its consumer-driven expectation to be nurtured by the church's staff for a humble desire to be an instrument of change destined to make an eternal difference. With submission to a God-inspired vision for service to the world, church members experience the Spirit's power moving in and through them to accomplish more for the kingdom than they could ever have imagined.

Chapter 10 details the three *support disciplines.* Together, they help to supply ministry servants with needed resources through a relevant and appropriate infrastructure. Specifically, this section explains how, when properly exercised, the support disciplines work:

• *Empowering systems* are a powerful means to encourage a church to exchange obsolete management strategies that promote control for streamlined ministry systems that help a church maximize its missional purpose. Well-crafted management guidelines for church life provide freedom for the Spirit's winds to blow in and through the church's people to accomplish great things for God.

• *Aligned facilities* are a powerful means to encourage church members to exchange a worldly mindset that church property is theirs for a biblical mindset that God is the rightful owner of all things. When faithful followers let God be God, the wind of the Spirit is at their backs and not in their faces.

• *Generous stewardship* is a powerful means to encourage a church to exchange the obligation of paying "club dues" for the joy of sharing God's blessings to make disciples of all nations. Congregational generosity is a common indicator of the presence of God's Spirit and is visible witness to a world yearning for meaning and significance.

Clearly, many ministry initiatives foster spiritual growth within a congregation, and my listing of congregational disciplines should not be taken as exhaustive. These habits do not make a congregation vital and alive, in the same way that the farmer does not make the corn grow. Rather, these activities till the soil of our collective hearts and encourage a readiness to cooperate with the Spirit's ongoing work in our lives. Apart from God's Spirit, a church—as well as the individual disciple—is impotent to let go of the world's values and embrace kingdom values. Following Christ demands a radical change of culture indeed. Congregational disciplines of the Church, therefore, help to create an environment in which the Spirit can more readily accomplish this needed transformation.

My Hopes for the Reader

Hope has always motivated me! Here's what I hope will come about as God's faithful people read and share this book:

First, I hope that as church leaders work through the book together, they will more clearly grasp that the primary issues of congregational faithfulness are always spiritual. Programs and theories have their place and role, but the collective attitude of our hearts toward Christ is the nonnegotiable starting point. Discipleship is a transferable and biblical model that clearly communicates this key truth.

Second, I hope readers will find the book concise without being simplistic. As a teacher and author, I strive to make complex matters understandable.

Third, I hope the text will help readers better understand the nature of spiritual transformation for themselves and the Church.

Fourth, I hope readers will more clearly understand what a faithful congregation looks and feels like. Unfortunately, many Christians have never tasted the saltiness of a Great-Commission–focused church that has prioritized the discipleship of the world.

Fifth, I hope my thoughts will instill in both congregations and individual disciples the desire to discern and take their next steps of faith. I can only hope the Spirit will use me to bless you as so many great Christian authors and teachers have blessed me and shaped the course of my own journey.

So there you have it: an easy-to-remember 3–D model—discipleship, dimensions, and disciplines—reveals the nature of personal transformation and the process of revitalizing the heart of your church. You'll learn about yourself and Christ's church at the same time! My prayers are with you as you proceed.

PART I

The Basics of Discipleship

Moving from Where We Have Been to Where We Are Called to Go

Discipleship is a process of exchanging a world where I (we) am at the center for a world where Christ is at the center. It is, therefore, a two-step process: we must leave our Egypt before we embrace God's promised land. Let's carefully explore the nature and dynamics of this exchange process.

1

Two Kingdoms

Polar Opposites

"I must preach the good news of the kingdom of God."

JESUS (Lk. 4:43a)

I am imagining a continuum.

Picture this: On one end, I can see the kingdom of God. Impossible, you say? Not if you spend any time reading the gospels, for the kingdom of God is the central focus of Jesus' teaching, preaching, and life. This kingdom enthrones God as its Ruler; God is at the center. As I look, I capture a vision of the Garden of Eden, God's world as originally intended.

At the other end of this spectrum, I can make out the kingdom of the world. There I am at the center, enthroned as the king of my own world. Visualizing this kingdom is easy. It is the culture of self-worship in which I have been raised and in which I have spent a great deal of time. This kingdom is the complete opposite of God's kingdom.

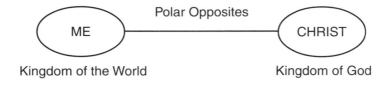

Kingdom of the World   Kingdom of God

For the sake of argument, let's say we are born in the center of my continuum. Which direction do we naturally gravitate toward during our early years? Which world is inherently more attractive to us? Which kingdom do we prefer deep down in our bones? The evidence is before us, and it's not pretty. We overwhelmingly prefer to live in a world in which we are at the center—the kingdom of the world. We delight in a culture that tells us to do things our way so that we can have it all—whatever "it" may be! In time, we move further and further away from God's design—some of us moving more quickly than others.

But a moment comes, in your life and mine, when we are confronted with the claims of the Gospel on our lives. We begin to recognize that a different way of living exists. God's world—with values completely foreign to our values—beckons us. We receive an invitation to move in the opposite direction, coming closer to God's kingdom by leaving behind our own—permanently. How permanent becomes painfully clear as we realize that leaving means dying to every inclination we have, every motive we harbor to protect and promote ourselves. Now, we must choose.

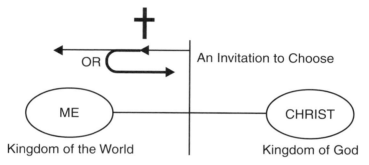

Those of us who respond "yes" to the invitation begin the process by turning. Not always quickly. Never easily. But a lifelong process of transformation starts as we increasingly let go of the world's ways and embrace the values of God's kingdom. Along the way, we learn what dying to self-determination and living a new life focused on Christ looks like. How long does the change take? A lifetime. What does this new lifestyle cost? Everything. What is such devotion called? Discipleship.

Disciple is the most common gospel term to describe those who accepted Jesus' invitation. Being a disciple is an ancient concept with

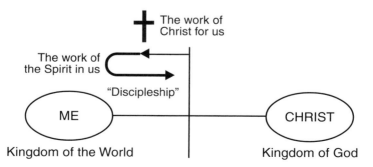

many modern connotations. Biblically, its primary meaning is to be a "learner," one guided by the Master Teacher. (Think of an apprentice learning valuable skills by working alongside a professional in the field.) Another Greek term for disciple means "to follow," and literally conveys the image of walking a well-worn path. As a result, a disciple of Christ deliberately forsakes old habits and adopts a lifestyle of learning and following.

Discipleship—for both the church and the individual—is *the process of exchanging a world in which we are at the center for a world in which God is at the center.* Get familiar with this definition. We will come back to it again and again in the course of this book. Before we proceed, however, let me reinforce one thing with which each church must grapple. Our daily steps of faith—our collective, face-to-face encounter with exchange—must begin with a painful question: "Whom do we choose as lord of our church life? Christ or ourselves?" As Jesus pointed out, denying always precedes following! The only way a congregation—or individual believer—can faithfully follow Christ and fulfill its mission-based calling is to *first* let go of the world's ways and *then* embrace Christ-like values. Congregational discipleship is a systemic change of priorities—a transformation of culture from us-centeredness to Christ-centeredness. Jesus conveyed these bedrock truths through first-century images and language. Let's revisit them in their biblical context and discover their dynamic equivalents in today's twenty-first–century world.

Jesus' Kingdom Focus

As children always do, my son Thomas has taught me a thing or two in his young life. Lately, I have been the student as I observe this 18-year-old fixate—or should I say focus?—on a single goal: mastering the ins and outs of his favorite video games. His focus takes on the added edge of persistence. In his drive to outwit the games, he returns again and again to his nemesis. No frustration or obstacle is too big for Thomas to engage as he wraps his hands around the game's controls.

My son's single-minded persistence reminds me of the focus of another Son—Jesus Christ. He had a mission and a message and deliberately went about His day-to-day life proclaiming both. No setting—or crowd—was too big or too small, too imposing or too unimportant for Him. His focus was on His message. His persistence was in the way he continually approached people. Jesus had a goal in mind: bringing the message of the kingdom of God to all who heard Him. He is still speaking today.

The gospels waste no time describing Jesus' eagerness to tell what He knew to be true. Mark introduces Jesus' mission with the words, "After

John was put in prison, Jesus went into Galilee, proclaiming the good news of God. 'The time has come,' he said. 'The kingdom of God is near. Repent and believe the good news!'" (1:14–15). Matthew tells us, "Jesus went throughout Galilee, teaching in their synagogues, preaching the good news of the kingdom, and healing every disease and sickness among the people" (4:23). Luke's account includes Jesus reading from the book of Isaiah in the synagogue at Nazareth. The passage from Isaiah (61:1, 2) depicts the coming of the kingdom of God. Jesus' response to the reading is His affirmation: "Today this scripture is fulfilled in your hearing" (Lk. 4:21).

Jesus refers to the kingdom early in His ministry and often thereafter. The phrase "kingdom of God" appears 126 times in the gospels! Even when the phrase is not specifically used, the focal point of Jesus' lessons and parables point to life in the kingdom. Jesus kept a kingdom focus always before Himself, from the very beginning of His ministry to His ascension.

The Kingdom Defined: What It Is

So, what exactly *is* the kingdom of God? Most simply, it is "the rule or reign of God,"[1] the way God's world operates, and the values that define such a world. To illustrate this point, consider the kingdom of Halley, where my wife Mary Lou and I rule or reign. Our "sovereign" domain is made of up that area in which we have a sphere of influence, which becomes pretty laughable when you consider that our domain includes three teenaged sons. The Halley kingdom is usually under the threat of being overthrown! Even so, our family has established a set of norms as to how we treat one another and how we divvy up household chores. All families have "kingdom" values that can be described and quantified for themselves and others.

A Modern Term for Kingdom: Organizational Culture

Social science provides us with a related term for kingdom, namely *organizational culture*. Edgar Schein, a lifelong student of organizations, describes culture as the "sum total of all the shared, taken-for-granted assumptions that a group has learned throughout its history."[2] In other words, culture is the "way things work around here" and is most visible in an organization's rituals, artifacts, and heroes. All human organizations—both large and small, new and old—have identifiable cultures that function as behavioral boundaries.

The kingdom of God can be understood as a type of culture. The clearest biblical example of this is the Garden of Eden (Gen. 1–2)–a succinct and clear image of God's ideal culture. Can you see Paul's fruit of the Spirit (Gal. 5:22, 23) that Adam and Eve exhibit prior to the fall? Can you see them living into the values of a kingdom community as described by Luke in the early chapters of Acts (esp. 2:42–47)? Indeed, "Where two or three are gathered in my name" is first exemplified in the Garden–a perfect kingdom culture.

Jesus–The Great Kingdom Communicator

Even though He didn't have the "advantages" of the electronic age, Jesus communicated His message brilliantly through stories, teachings, and personal example.

Stories

Jesus was the master storyteller! His stories offered wonderful insights about the kingdom of God. Most often he used parables, stories taken from everyday life to illustrate a central message. In the twenty-five or so parables recorded in the gospels, Jesus painted verbal pictures of the kingdom that His hearers could understand. The word *parable* literally means "to throw alongside." Essentially, Jesus used illustrations from everyday life and "threw them alongside" the spiritual realities of the kingdom so people could grasp His points based on what they knew to be true in their common experiences. A good parable is simple, under-standable, and unforgettable. The parable of the mustard seed (Mt. 13:31–32) conveys the central truth that the kingdom of God, though almost imperceptible today, will one day fill the earth. This parable shows a quantitative trait of the kingdom: *it is growing large.* The parables of the hidden treasure and the fine pearl (Mt. 13:44–46) illustrate the central truths that the kingdom of God is priceless and worth everything we own. These parables show a qualitative trait of the kingdom: *it is infinitely valuable.*

Formal Teaching

Jesus taught about the kingdom in a variety of settings. He was equally at home in the synagogue or out on a hillside–or even sitting in a boat on a lake! Jesus' Sermon on the Mount (Mt. 5–7) is considered by many to be His most complete instruction on the kingdom of God. Take a moment to read it and hear the Master Teacher at His best. This sermon begins with the well-known beatitudes that depict citizenship in God's kingdom as a combination of attitudes (right being) and attributes (right living).

Personal Example

Jesus Himself was the perfect model of kingdom citizenship. As he moved among the people–preaching, teaching, and healing–He reflected the values He taught and showed the beauty of a God-centered life. He walked His talk. The gospel accounts overflow with examples of Jesus doing ministry in perfect sync with His message. He validated the worth of a Samaritan, showing respect to a person subject to prejudice (Jn. 4). He demonstrated compassion by touching a leper, embracing a person subject to isolation (Mt. 8). He dispensed grace to a woman caught in adultery, offering mercy to a woman subject to harsh judgment (Jn. 8).

Jesus' life was filled with kingdom realities. Even as He would begin many of His parables with the words, "The kingdom of heaven is like…," *Jesus Himself* was that central message He was trying to convey to His listeners. That's what made Jesus such a great communicator: His life, message, and ministry were one.

The Kingdom of God vs. Its Polar Opposite– The Kingdom of the World

So why was Jesus so persistently focused in presenting His message about the kingdom of God? The reason is obvious: *The kingdom of the world–our world–is very different from God's kingdom.* Our three teenaged boys provide all the proof I need that major differences between the two kingdoms exist! My sons' natural tendencies are to live in a world in which they are at the center, not God. I see this in our kitchen. "What's for dinner?" is their collective cry as they tromp into the dining room, eager to help–you guessed it–themselves. They certainly do not come willing to cook, serve, or clean up!

Their behavior gets on my nerves. How can they be so selfish? But I have a mirror not far from the dining room table. When I glance into it, I see that my own motives and actions often reflect the same self-centeredness. Just last night, I failed to be an attentive listener to a spouse who had had a difficult day. I was too wrapped up in my own world and agenda. No wonder I can pinpoint my sons' faults so easily.

If I were not convinced of this reality within our own family–that is, our Halley organizational culture–I would only need to pick up our daily newspaper. Stories from around the globe reinforce the same perspective– our world is self-centric, not God-centric. Take a look at the most recent samplings I've read:

- A pregnant mother is murdered for her unborn child.
- A homosexual is beaten to death to satisfy the hatred of a fellow student.
- A widowed retiree is swindled out of her life's savings.
- A dictator keeps his people in poverty so he can enjoy a luxurious lifestyle.

• A prominent civic leader cheats on wife and family to bolster a middle-aged ego.

An even more penetrating proof of a "me-centered" preference comes alive every time I open my Bible. From beginning to end, the reality of our world's—and our own—rebellion and self-worship leaps from the pages. From then until now, the writer of Ecclesiastes has been correct: There is nothing new under the sun. I know that the kingdom of the world is alive and thriving, in constant tension with the kingdom that Jesus gave His life to show us.

Two Cultures: A Study in Contrasts

The more we dig into the gospels, the more we realize that Jesus, while focused and persistent, was also very courageous. He never pretended that God's culture and our earthly culture were even remotely alike. He never watered down His message to appease folks who disagreed with him. As a teacher, Jesus skillfully pointed out the vivid contrasts between the two kingdoms. In the Sermon on the Mount, Jesus declared that kingdom citizens are so different that they are salt and light to those around them. Just as salt adds flavor, preserves what it's sprinkled on, and draws out infection (when applied to a wound), and just as light pierces through darkness and is inviting, attractive, and unashamedly bright, so should kingdom citizens be. Jesus pointed out that as salt and light are irritants to their surroundings, so those who embrace His kingdom could expect ridicule and persecution for being countercultural. "If they persecuted me, they will persecute you also" (Jn. 15:20).

Not only did Jesus show the sharpness of kingdom contrasts in His teachings, He demonstrated that the values of the two worlds are actually inverted! Look through a glass prism, and what happens? Usually, you can see an upside-down image of what you expected. By using paradoxes—seeming contradictions—Jesus held up a prism and exposed the upside-down nature of what the world values as opposed to what He values:

• "So the last will be first, and the first will be last." (Mt. 20:16)
• "For whoever wants to save his life will lose it, but whoever loses his life for me and for the gospel will save it." (Mk. 8:35)
• "The greatest among you will be your servant." (Mt. 23:11)
• "For everyone who exalts himself will be humbled, and he who humbles himself will be exalted." (Lk. 14:11)

Even though Jesus' teachings were bold and different, they were not original in depicting the two-world distinctions. The Old Testament prophet Isaiah clearly drew a contrasting line:

"For my thoughts are not your thoughts,
  neither are your ways my ways," declares the LORD.
"As the heavens are higher than the earth,
  so are my ways higher than your ways
and my thoughts than your thoughts." (55:8–9)

Jesus spelled out exactly how His ways and thoughts differed from ours.

John and Paul: The Contrast Sharpened

Of all the gospel accounts, John's is most clear in highlighting stark kingdom differences. John points out the dualism between the "world above" and the "world below," also called "this world" (Jn. 8:23). John portrays one as needing to be "invaded" in order to be saved by the other. In this world, evil reigns with the devil as ruler (16:11), but Jesus is the light to those covered in darkness (12:46).

Indeed, John often uses the imagery of darkness and light as a way to highlight the difference between the kingdom of the world and God's kingdom. He associates darkness with "the world below" or "this world," and the light with "the world above." Jesus is the light (8:12) and has come to provide a way out of the dark (9:5; 11:9; 12:35; 12:46); the light shines in the darkness, and the darkness has not overcome it (1:5); finally, those who receive the light become sons and daughters of light (12:46).

Paul is anything but quiet on the subject of two worlds. His convictions come as no surprise, considering his life experiences before his encounter with the living Christ on the road to Damascus. (See Acts 7–9.) He is a prime example of a person claimed by the ruler of this world until Christ Jesus took hold of him. (See Phil. 3:12.) Even as he proclaims the reality of two kingdoms, Paul goes further and argues that people in this world have a clear preference, choosing self-rule over God's rule and reign. For Paul, a taste for the values of "this world" exposes an unhealthy appetite that even he cannot suppress. Paul's distressing drive to elevate and serve self over God rears its head even as he strives to claim his citizenship in God's kingdom:

> I do not understand what I do. For what I want to do I do not do, but what I hate I do. And if I do what I do not want to do, I agree that the law is good. As it is, it is no longer I myself who do it, but it is sin living in me. I know that nothing good lives in me, that is, in my sinful nature. For I have the desire to do what is good, but I cannot carry it out. For what I do is not the good I want to do; no, the evil I do not want to do–this I keep on doing. Now if I do what I do not want to do, it is no longer I who do it, but it is sin living in me that does it. (Rom. 7:15–20)

An Emerging Set of Truths about the World

Some years ago, Mary Lou and I were going out one evening. Quickly falling behind schedule, we were in a hurry; and neither of us likes to be late. As we tried to help Chuck, a toddler at the time, get dressed, he suddenly told us (with a perfect sense of timing) that he would get his own pants on, thank you very much. I will never forget his firm announcement: "I do myself! I do myself!" Those words pretty much sum up our human tendency, our strong preference, in fact, to usurp God and put ourselves in His rightful place. "I do myself," replaces, "Thy will be done." The scary part is that this choice of ours rears its head automatically, when we are very young. Chuck knew early on that he was the center of his world; he knew it innately. The challenge for him—as it is for all of us—is to let go of his desire to exalt himself and become a citizen for whom God's reign is sovereign.

As we conclude this chapter, let me highlight a few fundamental truths that will be key building blocks as we continue to explore the huge difference between "the world above" (where God reigns as King) and "the world below" (where we reside as king).

- *The kingdom of God is God-centered.* God is God, and we are not. This truth may seem obvious, but it is one that I seem to forget on an all-too-frequent basis!
- *The kingdom of the world is self-centered.* Apart from God, I am my own god, and the world revolves around me.
- *In Jesus' earthly ministry, He was passionate about revealing the kingdom of God.* Through stories, teachings, and example, Jesus opened the kingdom doors to everyone.
- *The values of the kingdom of God are diametrically opposed to the world we know best, the world in which we grew up.* God's ways are the opposite of ours.
- *Jesus is the model citizen of God's kingdom.* Everything He did and said reflects God's world perfectly.
- *All men and women are "model" citizens by birth in the kingdom of the world.* No one has to teach us to be selfish and self-centered; these traits are natural, and we are predisposed to be defiant and unyielding to God's ways.

On one occasion, a man called Jesus "good teacher." The Master's response was quick and to the point: "'Why do you call me good?' Jesus answered. 'No one is good—except God alone'" (Mk. 10:18). His response forced the man to rethink the nature of goodness, a nature that resides in God, not humans. We inherently reflect the ungodly world in which we live, but Jesus holds up both a mirror to show us who we are, and a prism to show us what He is like. What a contrast! The goal now is to take hold of the only truly effective remedy for crossing over from worldly citizenship to kingdom citizenship for both me, and us.

DISCUSSION QUESTIONS

Personal Discipleship

1. When did you first hear the gospel story of Jesus' life, death, and resurrection? How did you hear it? What convinced you to accept Christ's invitation to follow Him?

2. Since disciple means "learner" or "student," what have you been learning during the past year?

3. Who within your life best represents God's kingdom in the flesh? How?

4. Where within your world do you see the sharpest contrast between God's world and ours? Recent example?

5. If daily living in harmony with the kingdom of God and its values can be called perfect weather, how would you describe your current spiritual weather pattern?

Congregational Discipleship

1. How would you describe your congregation in light of the continuum imagery? Is the church's collective maturity best described as an infant, a toddler, a preschooler…a retiree?

2. What has your congregation been learning during the past year? Did one specific event prompt this growth? If so, what was it and why?

3. Describe the culture and values of the first church in which you were an active participant.

4. Where and in what ways does your church draw the sharpest contrast with the surrounding culture? Where does it most closely mirror the surrounding culture?

5. If daily living in harmony with the kingdom of God and its values can be called perfect weather, how would you describe your congregation's current spiritual weather pattern?

2

An Invitation to Exchange

Caught Between Two Worlds

"If anyone would come after me, he must deny himself and take up his cross daily and follow me."

JESUS (Lk. 9:23)

The old adage, "You can't have your cake and eat it too," is generally true–you have to come down on one side of an issue or the other, pure and simple. Since this wise saying is about food, let's stay on the subject and talk dieting. My favorite diet is the see-food diet: I see food, and I eat it! I am one of those folks who lives to eat rather than eats to live. Unfortunately, my pattern of eating too much cake recently caught up with me. For the past several years in a row, I have steadily gained two to three pounds a year, cursed by a slowing metabolism. As my weight has increased, my pants have been screaming for mercy. Hey, when your buttons start popping off, you know it's time for a change!

I faced a choice: I could keep going for the gusto and have a continued midriff crisis, or I could opt for a healthier diet and clothes that wouldn't cut off my blood supply. I decided to trade in one set of eating habits for another by exchanging my old love of sugar, bread, and pasta for a new love of protein, fruits, and vegetables. Several months later, I have decreased my waistline and increased my available wardrobe. But make no mistake: First I had to leave my old weighs–I mean *ways*–behind. Only then was I able to experience the payback on my scale and in my closet. To put it biblically, I had to exchange the "comforts" of Egypt for the benefits of the promised land!

The Source of Our Freedom to Choose

This personal vignette, while perhaps amusing, points to a certain truth about the process of exchanging one set of values for another. However, my dieting experience does not tell the whole story, as we consider the far more serious matter of exchanging a world in which I am at the center for a world in which Christ is at the center. Why? Because it implies that my choice revolved around *me* and *my decision* to lose weight. I had complete control, not only to choose my course of action but also to be chief negotiator between my meals and my wardrobe. At least for me, the source of my freedom to exchange was my own will power.

The freedom to become kingdom-of-God dwellers, however, depends on a totally different source—the power of God. The apostle Paul tells us, "When you were slaves to sin, you were free from the control of righteousness" (Rom. 6:20). In other words, without God's initiating grace we do not even have the privilege of exchanging one set of values for another. As worldly citizens, we are singularly focused on, enslaved to, and trapped by our own agenda. Fortunately, "while we were still sinners, Christ died for us" (Rom. 5:8b). Jesus—a servant to God's will—makes our escape from the prison of self-interest possible.

To the Galatians, Paul is adamant on this point: "It is for freedom that Christ has set us free" (Gal. 5:1a). Through Christ's work, we are truly free to chart a new course for our lives through faith. Through God's grace we are free to turn our backs on the world and its grip on our lives. Once we see that our choice begins with accepting this "amazing" grace, we can then fathom that the "new course" of exchanging me-centered values for God-centered values is nothing less than transformation at every level of our lives. This idea should not surprise us. Jesus suffered and died so we could be freed from our sins now, as well as for eternity.

To illustrate how God has secured our freedom to embrace His Son, let me recount a life experience that fellow baby-boomers can relate to: collecting Green Stamps! When I was growing up, my parents would get these special stamps for buying products at a variety of stores. At home, these stamps would be stored in a designated shoebox until it was overflowing. At that point, my mom would bribe my sister or me to begin the pasting process. The stamps were pasted into special Green Stamp books. Having learned the hard way that licking was only for novices, I would wet a sponge and begin. In time, a handful of books—full of stamps and bloated from moisture—were ready to be transported to the nearest, all-important "redemption center." Now this was no church, though we were pretty religious about showing up. No, the center was where the stamps could be redeemed or exchanged for something of equal value based on the number of books we unloaded.

Redemption literally means to "buy back," and that is exactly what God has done. Having been lost to sin through our arrogance and pride

(Gen. 3–11), we need freedom. God exchanges the precious blood of His Son, Jesus, for the freedom of our souls. (Calvary is the real redemption center!) The bottom line is this: God's costly grace guarantees our freedom and right to exchange our broken-down values for the hope and promise of the kingdom.

Transformation: A Costly Two-Step Process

Because we are hopelessly caught between two antithetical worlds, Jesus invites us to change directions and be transformed. Obviously, our Master Teacher knows that we need specific instructions on the nature of transformation. Over and over, His invitation reveals a two-step process: dying to our natural preference to have the world revolve around us, and living so that God is enthroned at the center of our world. Note carefully the process: *die* and *live*. Accepting Jesus' many invitations requires us to take not one, but two distinct and radical steps: *first,* we have to let go of our world and its ways; and *second,* we must embrace His kingdom and the values of God. No other effective avenue for transformation exists.

One of Jesus' best-known invitations is found in all three of the synoptic gospels: "If anyone would come after me, he must *deny himself* and take up his cross and *follow me.*" (Mt. 16:24; Mk. 8:34; Lk. 9:23; author's emphasis in this and subsequent passages.) On the heels of this invitation, Jesus, in all three passages, delivers another one: "For whoever wants to save his life will lose it, but whoever *loses his life* for me will *find it.*" *Denying + losing = dying* (to self at the center of my world). *Following + finding = living* (with God at the center of my world).

In John's Gospel, Jesus again illustrates the two steps of exchange but in a slightly different way. Those who accept His invitation need to understand that His message carries preconditions. "To the Jews who had believed him, Jesus said, '*If you hold to my teaching,* you are really my disciples. *Then you will know the truth,* and the truth will set you free'" (8:31–32). For me to know the truth, I must agree that the teachings of Christ are true and live by them. Jesus, wise Teacher that He is, will not let me have it both ways. Transformation only happens when I die to my old agenda so that I can live for God's agenda.

More Invitations Needing an RSVP

This same two-step idea is a recurring theme for Paul: "You were taught, with regard to your former way of life, to *put off* your old self, which is being corrupted by its deceitful desires;…and to *put on* the new self, created to be like God in true righteousness and holiness" (Eph. 4:22, 24). In other passages, Paul describes this process as a definite death-to-life progression, reversing the ugly trend we humans adopted from

Adam onward. "I have been *crucified with Christ* and I no longer live, but Christ lives in me. The life I live in the body, I *live by faith* in the Son of God, who loved me and gave himself for me" (Gal. 2:20). Only when we put things of "this world" to death can we clothe ourselves with a new nature, making us fit for life, true life, in the kingdom. "*Put to death,* therefore, whatever belongs to your earthly nature: sexual immorality, impurity, lust, evil desires and greed, which is idolatry…But now you must rid yourselves of all such things as these: anger, rage, malice, slander, and filthy language…*put on the new self,* which is being renewed in knowledge in the image of its Creator" (Col. 3:5, 8, 10).

Peter also understood the concept of trading old life for new in a very visceral way. Having lived through Jesus' death and resurrection, Peter intimately knew that the medium that makes exchange possible is none other than the Lord Himself. "He himself bore our sins in his body on the tree, so that we might *die to sins* and *live for righteousness;* by his wounds you have been healed" (1 Pet. 2:24).

When I summarized all the different ways the preceding passages describe the route to kingdom living, I was struck by their remarkably same message: two real steps have to occur. Choices define—and refine—our walk with Jesus.

Transformed Before Our Eyes

Whenever I see a butterfly, I think about the lengths God will go to get across His message of exchange, of dying so that we can live. The caterpillar—let's call it a pre-butterfly—spends most of its time eating and growing, but its skin does not grow. Consequently, it goes through a process of shedding and growing ever-larger exteriors. After it reaches its full size, it forms a protective shell around itself and, in time, reemerges as a beautiful butterfly. But what some people do not realize is that the majesty of the butterfly is always preceded by the "death" of the caterpillar. Once again, you have to leave Egypt before you get to the promised land.

Think about Jesus' words spoken shortly before His own death: "I tell you the truth, unless a kernel of wheat falls to the ground and dies, it remains only a single seed. But if it dies, it produces many seeds" (Jn. 12:24). He, the Master Biologist, spoke of a natural law concerning seeds to point to a larger, supernatural truth. We can only embrace life that produces fruit in the kingdom of God if we are willing to put to certain death our own "world below" tendencies and desires.

Group Dynamics: What's True for *Me* Is True for *Us*

Once we understand the grace-filled reality of our redemption and recognize Christ's two-step invitations to exchange our worldly culture for His kingdom culture, we discover yet another truth. We—the Church of Jesus Christ—also need to experience ongoing transformation. Our agenda must gradually give way to God's. Our self-centered norms must be exchanged for servant-centered values. I call this process *congregational discipleship*—a never-ending, cultural transformation.

The need for congregational discipleship should come as no surprise. If the Church is nothing more than the sum total of Jesus' disciples, what's true for every one of us individually must also be true for all of us collectively. The church is saddled with an enormous problem: people just like me. All of God's children are still in the process of growing up in the faith. Each of us embodies a unique blend of worldly and godly values. I'm not okay. We're not okay. But that *is* okay—God's grace is sufficient.

Just as with an individual experiencing transformation, a group of believers must grapple and come to terms with the very basic issue of values: do we embrace our home-grown, worldly values or God's? If you think the issue of value exchange is hard for just one devoted follower of Christ, just imagine the difficulty experienced by a whole congregation! That difficulty cuts right to the heart of why I have written this book. As believers, we have to deal with transformation at the deepest level. The call of Christ compels us, as His Body, to die to our way of doing things and to live so that His will is done through us. So, let us begin.

Making Kingdom Choices—The Hard Way

This principle of group discipleship shows itself even in the Old Testament. Remember my remark at the beginning of this chapter about having to leave Egypt before entering the promised land? I was referring to the very real exchange that the Israelites had to experience as they traded in the world and lifestyle they knew in Egypt for the kingdom God wanted to create through them in Canaan. As we look back on the story of their deliverance, we might think their exchange was easy. After all, weren't the Hebrews enslaved for four hundred years in Egypt? Wouldn't they be jumping for joy at the prospect of leaving a land of servitude and going to the country that God promised to Abraham as an "everlasting possession?" (Gen. 17:8) Apparently not! Very shortly after the Israelites witnessed the power of God displayed through both the plagues in Egypt (Ex. 7–11) and the Red Sea crossing (Ex. 14), they all-too-quickly recalled the "good" life—as slaves. Scripture describes their reluctance to exchange their self-centered world for a God-centered world: "In the desert the whole community grumbled against Moses and Aaron. The ["Back to Egypt Committee"] said to them, 'If only we had died by the LORD's hand in Egypt! There we sat around pots of meat and ate all the food we wanted, but you have brought us out into this desert to starve this entire assembly to death'" (Ex. 16:3). Unfortunately, Israel's preference for its own worldly culture proved to be a recurring pattern—interrupted only occasionally by seasons of faithfulness.

A New Testament Values Exchange: God's Grace Is for Everybody

A more encouraging story of group transformation occurs in the book of Acts. Some of Christ's early followers began telling the Gentiles that to be saved, they had to be circumcised. These followers found comfort in clinging to a set of values that made them members of an exclusive club instead of acknowledging that God's holy favor did not depend on an external ritual or heredity. Fortunately, the church leaders, many also Jewish themselves, were willing to deal with this issue head-on. Acts 15:5–11 records their wisdom. Peter clearly understood the group's need to exchange a worldly value—*exclusivity*—for a kingdom value—*equality*. (Acts 10 records how God transformed Peter's own attitude and understanding.) To follow Christ, the Church had to exchange the yoke of prideful people for the ways of a gracious God. To his everlasting credit, Peter died to the old wineskins of privileged status and lived for God's principles.

What a Modern-day Transformation Looks Like

Most of you have probably at least heard of Willow Creek Community Church, outside of Chicago. Begun in the mid-1970s with Bill Hybels as lead pastor, and sustained through the years by many dedicated staff and lay leaders, this church has devoted itself to living out the values of the New Testament Church. Of particular note is its commitment to reaching the lost—those in the surrounding community who have never heard or understood Jesus' invitation to be redeemed and transformed. Though some may disagree with the church's methodologies, few deny the spiritual vitality of Willow Creek's ministry. In the process of making the Great Commission a priority, this congregation has experienced a real transformation. Because spreading the good news of the gospel is such a large priority, this community of faith has deliberately gone through some exchanges of its own so that God's work can be done. Every weekend, Willow Creek holds a number of services tailored to the needs, tastes, and time convenience of the nonmembers. That's right; these "seeker-friendly" services are meant for those who are mainly unchurched. So when do the members of Willow Creek come to "traditional" worship services to be built up in the faith? On weeknights!

As we think about how unusual this arrangement may sound, let's consider what folks who belong to Willow Creek Community Church are willing to exchange. These members understand that going to a church that takes seriously its call to bring others into the fold means inconvenience. It means rearranging hectic mid-week schedules so they can worship God. It means letting go—yes, *dying*—to the preference of going to church on Sunday, the way they had always done before, and embracing—yes, *living*—to the value of making room in their hearts and in their church for others who need Christ.[1] Willow Creek is just one example of a church willing to accept Jesus' invitation to exchange a world in which it is at the center for a world in which God is at the center. Other churches that also engage in congregational discipleship understand that the Holy Spirit works powerfully only when they choose to lay down their own agendas to follow God's agenda. These communities give us a glimpse of what God desires for His redeemed Church. In Parts Two and Three we will explore at length the forms of discipleship they embrace collectively.

An Emerging Set of Truths about His Invitation and Our Choice

In the early 1970s in Alexandria, Virginia, the Titans, a group of racially mixed high school football players thrown unexpectedly together, found themselves caught between two antithetical worlds. On one end of the spectrum was the world of hatred and prejudice. Each team member, black as well as white, was raised in this world and had grown to expect it. As fall practice began, the players demonstrated their preference to stay bound to the beliefs and behaviors they grew up with. On the other end of the spectrum was a world that few had experienced or could even imagine. In this world, racial equality and mutual respect were the dominant values. In the midst of these polar opposites, Herman Boone—the new black coach of the Titans—invited his players to let go of their bigotry and embrace teamwork. (The Disney movie *Remember the Titans* recounts this inspirational story.)

Like many cities at the time, Alexandria was going through a forced desegregation process that had left both blacks and whites defensive, angry, and hostile. Within this context, the school board made a number of politically motivated decisions, including one to hire a new football leader, Coach Boone. The prior coach of the high school, Bill Yost—a successful white man who was well liked in the community—predictably found this a bitter pill to swallow. With the loyal white parents and players prepared to bolt, this former leader agreed to be an assistant to the new coach—at least for the upcoming year. From the outset of the summer football training camp, Coach Boone could see that he actually had two teams: a white one and a black one. During the first weeks, he repeatedly attempted to get his players to accept one another, but his initial efforts were quickly rejected. Then, early one morning, he woke the players and led them through a difficult and grueling run in the nearby woods. After hours of exhausting effort, the players arrived at a famous Civil War battlefield: Gettysburg. With passion and conviction, Coach Boone reminded his players of the 50,000 men who had died there over 100 years earlier over the same issues. He then challenged them to die to hatred and prejudice and to adopt the attitudes of a unified team.

On that day, the transformation began, led by two key players—one white, one black. Barriers that had previously divided the team began to crumble. The example of these two respected young men provided the impetus for other players to let go of the distrust and animosity of their Egypt and embrace the equality and teamwork of the team's promised land. Even as the players returned to Alexandria and faced the racial mistrust and hatred embraced by their parents and peers, these young men never lost sight of the new world they chose to embrace at the training camp. As the team stuck together throughout the fall, they compiled a stunning record of wins, ending in a perfect season and the state championship title. But even more, they awakened their town to the possibilities that exist when people are ready to exchange worlds.

The promised land of God's world is so appealing—Jesus' "abundant life" here on earth followed by participation in God's eternal kingdom. But the cost is exceedingly high—my transformation, which must begin with a death: my own. To experience God's best, I must leave the Egypt of my self-serving priorities and embrace His servant-minded values. To be transformed and experience God's blessings, we, the Church, must also walk the same path.

The deeper I go, the more I know I am just beginning to plumb the awesome depths of our Heavenly Parent's principles for genuine spiritual transformation for both the individual and the Church. The following truths provide additional building blocks so we can begin to grasp the meaning of being Christ's loyal disciples, both individually and corporately.

- *Our freedom to be kingdom citizens is a result of God's initiating grace and Christ's redemptive work.* You and I are loved by God more than we can ever imagine!
- *Having opened our eyes to God's world and its benefits, Jesus invites us to refocus our lives on our Heavenly Parent rather than on ourselves.* His invitation demands, however, that we let go of our broken world and its ways and embrace the kingdom and its values.
- *Transformation isn't easy.* To live you have to choose to die. Only you can decide if the prize is worth the process, which is filled with struggles and perseverance.

- *The principles of individual spiritual transformation are also true for the church.* Congregational discipleship involves the deliberate exchange of values—or cultures—just as individual discipleship does.

Jesus says, "Here I am! I stand at the door and knock. If anyone hears my voice and opens the door, I will come in and eat with him, and he with me" (Rev. 3:20). In other words, your invitation to exchange is in His hand. He is beckoning you to travel the path of lifelong discipleship. What will be your response?

DISCUSSION QUESTIONS

Personal Discipleship

1. Spiritual transformation is described as a two-step process that combines letting go of worldly values and embracing godly ones. What is an example from your past journey of faith that exemplifies this process?

2. What worldly value is the most difficult for people in our culture to let go of? What's your proof?

3. In the recent past, in what aspect of your life have you been hearing God's call to be transformed?

4. Why do you think that the term "disciple" has come to be identified with "super-Christians" rather than as a synonym for Christian?

5. What aspect of Jesus' discipleship expectations is most challenging for you?

Congregational Discipleship

1. Spiritual transformation is described as a two-step process that combines letting go of worldly values and embracing godly ones. What example from your church's history exemplifies this process?

2. What worldly value is the most difficult for most congregations to let go of? What is your proof?

3. In what aspect of the church's life has the leadership recently been hearing God's call to be transformed?

4. In the original biblical language, the term *disciple* most often appears in the plural form even as it is used almost exclusively to refer to individual believers. What might explain this inconsistency?

5. What aspect of Jesus' discipleship expectations is most challenging for your congregation?

PART II

The Five Dimensions of Congregational Discipleship

What We Can Expect along the Way

Having established spiritual transformation as a process of exchange that involves two distinct steps, we now turn our attention to describing what a radical change of values looks like for the individual and the Body of Christ. Five dimensions—*ongoing, relative, purposeful, contentious,* and *cooperative*—describe the foundation for changing from a kingdom of the world culture to a kingdom of God culture.

Let us begin to examine these dimensions and their vital contributions to our spiritual transformation.

3

An Ongoing Process

Are We There Yet?

"But everyone who hears these words of mine and does not put them into practice is like a foolish man who built his house on sand. The rain came down, the streams rose, and the winds blew and beat against that house, and it fell with a great crash."

JESUS (Mt. 7:26–27)

Patience may be a virtue, but in the twenty-first century, it looks more like a dinosaur: virtually extinct! Many of us want what we want *now,* which really stands for No Other Way: not later, not tomorrow, but *now.* My guess is that we want our dose of "religion" now, too. Wouldn't it be great to cozy up to our computers, dial up *www.Jesus.com,* click on the Discipleship icon, then click on Personal, and then select the menu option entitled "immediately completed"? *Voila!* We are changed instantly into a combination of Mother Teresa and Billy Graham, ready to take on the world, our family obligations, our in-laws, and our jobs! If my transformation were only that easy! But it is not. Jesus never expected it to be. Discipleship is ongoing–a lifelong process for both the individual Christian and the Body of Christ, bearing no resemblance to a "now" mindset, or even to a "then" mindset. Here's what discipleship is not: a decision; a timed and dated event; an isolated, life-changing experience that happened some years ago; or even a certain span of years when God seemed nearby.

Discipleship, conveniently or not, has little use for our speed, efficiency, or now-ness. Rather, it is a lifestyle of faithfulness fueled by God's grace and the way we live our lives–relying on Christ–on a daily, *ongoing* basis. The Bible has a lot to say about walking with God in faithfulness–discipleship–as an ongoing process. Let's look more closely and consider the implication for both the individual believer and the Church.

Personal Discipleship: Don't Stop Now...Keep Going!

One of my seminary mentors, Bob Tuttle, used to say—and probably still does—that being a disciple is like riding a bike: you're either moving forward or most likely falling off. The point is that following Christ demands that we stay engaged in a process. Can you imagine Jesus calling us to follow him for only a season of our lives? "Come to me—*for a couple of months or as long as you want*—all you who are weary and burdened, and I will give you rest. Take my yoke upon you...*for whatever time frame works for you*...and learn from me, for I am gentle and humble in heart, and you will find rest for your souls." Or how about this? "If you hold to my teaching...*with strong conviction for several weeks after a mountaintop experience*...you are really my disciples. Then you will know the truth, and the truth will set you free." Let's take a moment to see what Jesus really said.

A Direct Message

Jesus never believed or taught that discipleship was a short-term commitment. Remember, He knew that his followers would take up His ministry and message and accomplish even "greater things that these" (Jn. 14:12). He also knew that they would fail if they didn't consistently keep their eyes, and hearts, focused on Him. His words, "Take my yoke upon you and learn from me, for I am gentle and humble in heart, and you will find rest for your souls" (Mt. 11:29), and "anyone who does not take his cross and follow me is not worthy of me" (Mt. 10:38), imply a lifetime devotion, not a one-time decision. Taking on a yoke or picking up a cross means shouldering over the long haul.

In delivering His message that true disciples must persevere, Jesus frequently uses the imagery of fruit. The disciples' long-term fruitfulness is, in fact, a sign that they are abiding in Him and bringing honor to His Father. Describing the Father's painful (for us) yet necessary (for Him) act of pruning, Jesus says: "He cuts off every branch in me that bears no fruit, while every branch that does bear fruit he trims clean so that it will be even more fruitful...This is to my Father's glory, that you bear much fruit, showing yourselves to be my disciples" (Jn. 15:2, 8). Finally, Jesus reveals that the nature of persistent fruit-bearing—the qualities of kingdom living best detailed by Paul in Galatians 5:22, 23—rests in the grace of God and brings forth eternal results: "You did not choose me, but I chose you and appointed you to go and bear fruit—fruit that will last. Then the Father will give you whatever you ask in my name" (Jn. 15:16).

Jesus is blunt and to the point: we are to produce fruit—beautifully (qualitative) and abundantly (quantitative). His numerous references to persistent, season-after-season fruitfulness strongly suggest that our walk of faith is just that—an ongoing walk, not just an occasional, random step. After all, who would want fruit that is only half ripe?

Are You Really, Really Sure?

Jesus took the call to discipleship so seriously that He challenged His followers to count the cost carefully before even joining Him. He saw no reason for people to embark on a lifelong path unless they intended to complete the journey. If you've had your fill of fruit imagery, turn your attention to what Jesus taught about construction. While you're at it, notice that Jesus puts up a red flag on the work zone—Caution, the half-hearted need not apply: "Suppose one of you wants to build a tower. Will he not first sit down and estimate the cost to see if he has enough money to complete it? For if he lays the foundation and is not able to finish it, everyone who sees it will ridicule him, saying, 'This fellow began to build and was not able to finish'" (Lk. 14:28–30). Jesus also points out the folly of thinking you're a fully-formed disciple when you fail to invest the equity time and energy to lay a firm foundation:

> "Therefore everyone who hears these words of mine and puts them into practice is like a wise man who built his house on the rock. The rain came down, the streams rose, and the winds blew and beat against that house; yet it did not fall, because it had its foundation on the rock. But everyone who hears these words of mine and does not put them into practice is like a foolish man who built his house on sand. The rain came down, the streams rose, and the winds blew and beat against that house, and it fell with a great crash." (Mt. 7:24–27)

In case we haven't already gotten the point, Jesus tells us one more time, using that common, everyday spice that is useful *only as long as it retains its goodness*: "Salt is good, but if it loses its saltiness, how can it be made salty again? It is fit neither for the soil nor for the manure pile; it is thrown out. He who has ears to hear, let him hear" (Lk. 14:34–35).

Emerging Truth about My Discipleship

Over the years, I have been privileged to be around a handful of disciples whose persistence in faith is nothing short of remarkable. A recent example is Beth—a wife and mother of two teenage boys. Beth's back is not right and, unless God intervenes, never will be again. Her pregnancies revealed a congenital problem with her spine, and pain is a daily reminder of her limitations. Not long ago, Beth barely survived her fifth major surgical procedure. (She has had over thirty surgeries for related issues.) This particular operation was a twelve–hour process in which titanium rods and cages were used to rebuild some of her discs. Need I say more?

Predictably, Beth currently spends many hours in bed. So, how would you respond to these circumstances? Would your faith be ongoing, or would you be tempted, like me, to be angry and bitter? I am sure she has her moments; but whenever I am with her, I am the one that is encouraged. Witnessing her persistence in running the race of faith is powerful.

Christ does not invite us to follow Him for just a season of our lives until another, more important, set of priorities emerges. Remember His invitation? Well, our RSVP requires an ongoing, persistent, and fruit-filled restructuring of our lives. Day after day–like Beth–we need to commit ourselves to walk by faith, striving mightily to not swerve off the path. As we gain greater clarity about our journeys, the following principles will help guide us:

- *Jesus, using various metaphors which His listeners could grasp, repeatedly spoke of faithfulness as an ongoing process.* Jesus' many discussions of ample and appropriate fruit point to the ripeness and goodness of persistent, productive discipleship.
- *Jesus cautioned His disciples to count the cost before embarking on the journey.* He issued this stern warning for a reason: The walk of faith will cost everything.

Congregational Discipleship

The Church of Jesus Christ also needs to assess the high expectation of remaining faithful and fruitful day after day. By reviewing the teaching of the Scriptures, we gain a better understanding of how discipleship is an ongoing transformational process for us as well.

God's Absolute Precondition

The Old Testament describes the story of Israel's struggle to be faithful on an ongoing basis. Not surprisingly, Israel's story is a roller coaster ride full of ups and downs. God's chosen people experienced periods of great obedience and trust, which were then followed by extended times of stubborn resistance. Through it all, we clearly see that God's expectations regarding faithfulness are constant. The Holy One calls the people to be persistent. Walking with the Creator is clearly portrayed as a lifestyle, not just a one-time, initial commitment. From the outset, God–through Moses–clearly states: "If you pay attention to these laws and are careful to follow them, then the LORD your God will keep his covenant of love with you, as he swore to your forefathers" (Deut. 7:12). There are to be no misunderstandings. God's covenant relationship with Israel had a nonnegotiable precondition: the people were to follow the laws and decrees day after day.

But what about the inevitable mistakes that Israel would make? God further clarifies for His people the nature of His expectations: "The LORD,…the compassionate and gracious God, [is] slow to anger, abounding in love and faithfulness, maintaining love to thousands, and forgiving wickedness, rebellion and sin" (Ex. 34:6–7a). We see from these words that God does not expect perfection and is patient with mistakes. With additional reading of God's laws, we even discover specific provisions for unfaithfulness in a system of sacrificial offerings. But even within these grace-filled decrees, a definite limit exists—the nature of prophecy consistently combines promise and warning.

Just before Israel entered the promised land, God sternly communicated the conditions for continuing to enjoy God's gracious covenant with clear warnings. (See Deut. 29:18, 22, 24–28.) Unfortunately, the reality of these warnings are borne out in history, recounted by the Old Testament's prophetic books. God's words speak for themselves: "They have returned to the sins of their forefathers, who refused to listen to my words. They have followed other gods to serve them. Both the house of Israel and the house of Judah have broken the covenant I made with their forefathers" (Jer. 11:10). God's patience—though bountiful—ran out as day after day the community failed to exercise faith. In short, Israel forgot the huge importance of maintaining an ongoing, fruitful relationship with its covenant-making God.

New Testament Examples: The Seven Churches of Revelation

The early chapters of the Book of Revelation provide us with great insights about obstacles to ongoing faithfulness for first-century congregations. Revelation 2–3 preserve seven letters from Christ to various congregations in Asia that serve as a rich resource for better understanding congregational discipleship. The context of these congregations is very significant. Let me summarize a few important points. *First,* the central challenge facing these churches was to remain faithful in the midst of a pagan Roman society. As we shall see, these churches and others like them existed in a hostile environment that had little patience for their belief in Christ, a belief judged as quite countercultural at that time. *Second,* the arrival of the Roman Empire in the first century B.C.E. was greeted by most with genuine gratitude. Its economic and legal stability ushered in a time of peace, prosperity, and freedom for most. However, by the time of the Revelation, Rome and its leadership had developed into a new and mandatory religious order that dictated worshiping the emperor—a direct conflict for those who were loyal to Jesus. *Third,* the influence of emperor worship was downright dangerous for John—the probable author of Revelation—and he was alarmed for the Asian churches as well. This new cult had become so pervasive within the economic and political structures that faithful disciples were not able to live out their persistent commitment to Christ safely.

In reading these seven letters, I am convinced that Jesus is in touch with the needs, challenges, and reality of these congregations. The phrase "I" appears over 50 times in these 51 verses. Jesus is not sequestered on some faraway cloud, oblivious to the churches' day-to-day struggles. He is present, active, involved, and knowing:

> "I know your deeds, your hard work and your perseverance. I know that you cannot tolerate wicked men, that you have tested those who claim to be apostles but are not, and have found them false." (to Ephesus, 2:2)

> "I know your afflictions and your poverty—yet you are rich! I know the slander of those who say they are Jews and are not, but are a synagogue of Satan." (to Smyrna, 2:9)

See also Jesus' words to the churches at Pergamum (2:13), Thyatira (2:19), Sardis (3:1b), Philadelphia (3:8), and Laodicea (3:15).

Based on his firsthand knowledge, Jesus challenges, promises, threatens, predicts, rebukes, praises, judges, counsels, loves, and disciplines these congregations. Let's look at His words, which will better help us understand His perspective on the need for ongoing faithfulness. Each of the letters in Revelation generally follows the same basic pattern: Jesus identifies Himself as the author, acknowledges the church and its particular circumstances, provides commendations for faithfulness, identifies areas of needed growth, challenges the community of faith to grow, and promises rewards if it does. As a result, we can easily see Jesus' expectation for ongoing faithfulness.

- *First,* He compliments most of the churches for enduring and persevering:

    > "Since you have kept my command to endure patiently, I will also keep you from the hour of trial that is going to come upon the whole world to test those who live on the earth." (to the Philadelphians, 3:10)

    > "You have persevered and have endured hardships for my name, and have not grown weary." (to the Ephesians, 2:3)

- *Second,* He calls most to repent for their collective sin—a clear implication that faithfulness is not an event, but a lifestyle of following:

"Remember the height from which you have fallen! Repent and do the things you did at first. If you do not repent, I will come to you and remove your lampstand from its place." (to the Ephesians, 2:5)

- *Third,* in all seven letters He promises rewards for those "who overcome" (2:7, 11, 17, 26; 3, 5, 12, 21), not just to those who have at one time participated in an act or event of following Christ. Of particular note are His comments to the church at Laodicea. In the midst of a well-to-do industrial community, this congregation has become increasingly satisfied, complacent, and apathetic—a reality that disgusts Christ. His correspondence leaves no doubt about the spiritual risk the congregation is incurring by its actions: "I know your deeds, that you are neither cold nor hot. I wish you were either one or the other! So, because you are lukewarm—neither hot nor cold—I am about to spit you out of my mouth." (3:15–16)

Throughout biblical history—from God's call for Israel to Christ's commands for the New Testament Church—faithfulness, the following of God's kingdom path, is an ongoing action. Endurance and persistence are the genuine hallmarks of discipleship.

Reverse Discipleship—What Happens When a Church Stops Pedaling

Let's revisit the "bicycle of faith," the idea that we have to keep persistently peddling if we don't want to fall flat on our spiritual faces. As we have seen in the Scriptures, it is quite a challenge to keep letting go of our "Egypt" and taking transformational steps of faith toward God's "promised land." Over the centuries, many people have tried to understand why some churches persistently embrace kingdom priorities and others do not. Many have noted that the early years of a congregation's life are frequently marked by faithfulness and spiritual vitality. Within ten years, however, the vast majority of churches lose their kingdom focus and enter a period of extended decline, while the minority remain healthy. Why do so many churches tend to fail after starting out with such strength and commitment?

Alan C. Klaas's book *In Search of the Unchurched* records the results of an extensive Lutheran study called the Church Membership Initiative, which sought to answer this very question by isolating the variables that distinguish a growing church from one in decline. Klass and his colleagues found that the growing churches they studied—only about 20 percent of the total studied—view themselves in terms of mission to *nonmembers.* These communities take seriously the "Great Commission" focus of bringing the good news to those who have never heard it while continuing to preach, teach, and beseech members to grow in their faith and commitment. However, the great majority of churches have forsaken their initial kingdom purpose and now define themselves only in terms of ministry to *current members*. These communities are slowly but surely spiraling downward, both in growth and in effective ministry.[1]

Note carefully what happens to the unhealthy churches. They turn away from a church culture in which God's agenda—reaching the world beyond the walls with the gospel—is central. Instead, they embrace a church culture in which their own agenda is central. These churches practice reverse discipleship! They supplant God's world for their own, just like Adam and Eve did. The predictable result? Spiritual decline. This downward spiral, however, is only the symptom of an underlying issue.

The Real Cog in the Wheel

These unfaithful churches experience a systemic or root problem: Jesus is no longer Lord and Head of their congregations. It's that simple, and that deadly. Any church that claims to follow Christ must be willing to claim His values as well. Jesus' values are very clear: Deny yourself. Follow me. Lose your life. Be last. And here's the real rub: Jesus clearly tells his disciples, "If you love me, you will obey what I command" (Jn. 14:15). A church that does not make Christ its Lord to the point of obeying God's commands will not actively seek out those who are lost. That church will not embrace the Great Commission as its defining purpose because that church is too comfortable with enthroning itself and ignoring the call to make disciples. Ongoing congregational discipleship requires ongoing obedience to the Creator.

Emerging Truths about Our Discipleship

The reality of exchanging our world for God's is that we must do our utmost to keep the ongoing nature of discipleship front and center. Otherwise, a church can lose its zeal and enthusiasm for the Gospel. It will stop pedaling, fall off its bicycle, and come crashing to the ground. (Reverse discipleship is much easier to live out than faithful discipleship.) As we see in the struggling churches in Revelation 2 and 3, the challenges to faithfulness run the full gamut. At times, we find the obstacles of the surrounding culture to be overwhelming and discouraging. At others times, we simply grow comfortable and complacent after a few years of success. The biblical witness, though, shakes us up and plainly shows us that ongoing discipleship is a necessary ingredient if we desire citizenship in God's kingdom.

As we proceed, the following principles will help to shape our perspective on the Church:

- *The Bible repeatedly speaks of faithfulness as an ongoing process for God's people.* From Israel to the Church, we are to keep pedaling.
- *Like Jesus' followers, Israel—God's chosen—is advised to count the cost before adopting His covenant.* God's abundant promises are conditioned upon the faithfulness of His people over time.
- *Numerous warnings are given to groups of followers who tire of being faithful.* Moses, in the Old Testament, and Jesus Himself, in Revelation, are particularly clear. They expect God's people to exhibit enduring faith.
- *Today's churches must also guard against becoming too complacent.* Again and again, congregations must acknowledge that Christ is Lord in order to faithfully exchange a world in which they are at the center for a world in which God is at the center.

DISCUSSION QUESTIONS

Personal Discipleship

1. The early part of John 15 records Jesus' strong emphasis on "remaining" faithful. Brainstorm other synonyms for this concept and reread the passage with the new terms. What new insights emerge in the process?

2. If Jesus were to teach today on counting the cost of discipleship (Mt. 7), what contemporary illustrations might Jesus use to make this same point?

3. Identify an example of a life experience that has challenged the persistence of your faith. What made it particularly difficult?

4. What is the greatest contemporary threat to most Christians' ongoing faith?

5. What is the greatest threat to your faithfulness?

Congregational Discipleship

1. Based on your understanding, what were the reoccurring factors that undermined Israel's ongoing faithfulness?

2. What are the factors that you see commonly derailing the health of the local church?

3. What parallels do you see between the Church's struggle to be persistent and other human organizations?

4. Identify examples of times when your church lost sight of the kingdom of God. Is there any pattern to these circumstances?

5. What is the greatest threat to your church's persistent faithfulness?

4

A Relative Process

The Journey Starts Here

We do not dare to classify or compare ourselves with some who commend themselves.

PAUL (2 Cor. 10:12a)

Consider "Big John": He's one of those people at my local YMCA who doesn't need a last name for identification! His claim to fame is sheer body mass. In fact, at 6 ft. 4 in. and 240 lbs., he's not only huge; he's one strong dude, lifting as much as 370 lbs. of weights.

Consider Halil Mutlu: He is a weightlifter from Turkey who won an Olympic gold medal. If you are imagining some hulking behemoth like John, forget it. Halil weighs only 122 lbs., no joke. He is one of only three weightlifters to have ever lifted three times his own body weight—a total of 370 lbs. in competition.

Consider Charlie Halley: I weigh 150 pounds before ice cream. Lifting three times my body weight would find me hoisting 450 pounds. Are you kidding? Halil Mutlu has achieved a stunning goal, and, pound for pound, he is one of the strongest men ever.

My point is this: exchanging a world in which I am at the center for a world in which Christ is at the center—discipleship—is like weightlifting. Progress and achievement are strictly relative. Following Jesus is a *unique* journey of faith for me as well as for the community of faith, Christ's Church. Though our paths can appear similar at various junctures, the differences are significant and striking: we are God's distinctive creations, our past histories are never identical, and our interpretations of these life experiences are always quite personal. As a result, our next steps of faith—as illumined by our Creator's prodding Spirit—are reflections of where we are on our own journey.

This chapter explores the second of the five dimensions of discipleship—its *relative* nature. The Bible has much to say about faithfully walking with God as a relative process. Let's look more closely and consider the implication for both the individual believer and the Church.

Personal Discipleship
Abraham's Incredible—But Not First—Step of Faith

If you begin your study of Abraham's life in Genesis 22, you will most likely conclude that Abraham, as well as God, was either crazy, deluded, or both. Why would anyone even consider sacrificing his son? What kind of a god would even ask it? This demand by God and Abraham's response, however, are understandable only in light of their previous dealings with one another. You see, the first twenty-one chapters of Genesis teach us that God is worthy of Abraham's trust. In the very beginning, God expresses goodness through a marvelous creation and grace-filled design for life. Later in Genesis, God repeatedly blesses Abraham and even rescues him from consequences that stemmed from his disappointing lapses in faith. For many years, the Holy One persistently and patiently guides Abraham and his family, culminating in the birth of Abraham's son, something so outrageously beautiful and unexpected that the child is named Isaac, meaning *he laughs*. Abraham had come to see and recognize that all he had bespoke of a loving, faithful God. After many years of relationship and faith-building, God tests Abraham by asking him to give up his son Isaac and return him to God. Grounded in God's proven faithfulness, and in spite of his most profound fears, Abraham responds relative to his own life experience and obeys.

Jesus the Gauntlet-Thrower: This One's for You

The gospels also clearly demonstrate God's unique ability to tailor discipleship invitations so that they confront people precisely at their points of resistance. Let's examine how Jesus' razor-sharp accuracy pierced through hard hearts, peered at the relative stumbling blocks littering paths of faith, and pointed out the attitudes or actions in need of radical change.

WEALTH

Consider the rich young man who wondered what he needed to do to attain eternal life. To this person of wealth and worldly confidence, Jesus said, "Go, sell everything you have and give to the poor, and you will have treasure in heaven. Then come, follow me" (Mk. 10:21). Jesus knew that material possessions had a grip on the soul of this particular young man. Understanding that people cannot worship God and Mammon simultaneously, Jesus told the man exactly what he needed to do to remain a disciple: He had to let go of his "stuff" so he could freely grasp the life Jesus offered him.

Family Ties

Consider the devoted family men who aspired to be disciples. Jesus challenged them to stay focused on the kingdom, rather than on their loved ones:

> But the man replied, "Lord, first let me go and bury my father." Jesus said to him, "Let the dead bury their own dead, but you go and proclaim the kingdom of God." Still another said, "I will follow you, Lord; but first let me go back and say good-by to my family." Jesus replied, "No one who puts his hand to the plow and looks back is fit for service in the kingdom of God." (Lk. 9:59–62)

For these men, Jesus recognized that perhaps family ties were the relative cords that were strangling them spiritually. Accordingly, Jesus called them to rethink their priorities so they could seek first the kingdom of God.

Relative Confusion—The Problem of Inferiority

Even today, Jesus beckons us—his modern-day followers—to deeper levels of discipleship. Unfortunately, many Christians do not understand the principle that Christ knows them, loves them, and prods them based on their relative journeys with Him. They easily become bogged down as they compare themselves to others. At times, I have been discouraged by reading Christian biographies because I compared what I considered my pathetic walk of faith to the glowing images of faithfulness portrayed on the pages of these books. This struggle with inferiority should come as no surprise. James Dobson, a well-respected Christian psychologist, has observed that insecurity among adolescents is a universal experience and primarily a function of two key issues: intelligence and external appearance.[1] My personal experiences, both as a teen and as a youth pastor, bear out this truth. But here's the rub: inferiority is always *relative* to someone else. I only draw conclusions about myself after I look at those around me. Am I as smart as my peers? Am I as attractive or as athletic as my friends? Most, if not all of us, are haunted by these questions. The result is a sure and steady erosion of our self-worth. It's no different for many Christians.

Valid Comparisons—Using the Right Compass

So, how do I chart my progress as a disciple? How do I know if I am moving further away from our fallen world and closer to a Christ-centered world? Am I convinced that I am moving in the right direction, or am I at a standstill, lost and confused? I would suggest two things: *first,* get rid of the urge to map your faithfulness according to what you see someone else doing; *second,* grab the right tool, the accurate compass, to plot your continuing journey. Specifically, measure yourself against two persons: yourself and Jesus. Here's how the compass works. When I compare myself to me, I can see if I am making progress over time. Exchanging worlds–the essence of discipleship–means transformation in both my attitudes and actions. I should be able to see tangible changes in my life, as I did the day I became a Christian. The night before, I had "borrowed" a Continental Trailways chrome eagle off the church camp bus. My quick remorse–following on the heels of giving my life to Christ–told me that my spiritual compass was pointing in the right direction. I was already changing from the outside in.

More typically, however, we measure progress as more evolutionary than revolutionary. With the perspective of months and years, and with the guidance of hindsight, we can observe and marvel at God patiently at work, helping us die to the world and live for Christ. Over time, I expect to see evidence of the Spirit's transformational power if I am cooperating.

Here's the other way the compass works. When I compare myself to Jesus, I never fall into the trap of complacency or arrogance, at least not for long! I dare not rest on the laurels of my own faithfulness as measured against only myself. If I do, I quickly stagnate, stewing in my meager accomplishments, while Jesus uses the compass point to prick and prod me to a higher level of discipleship. So much for self-righteousness! Jesus is the ultimate standard, the true course-setter, for our lifestyle. We are called to increasingly reflect the qualities of Christ in our daily lives. Paul is clear on this subject: "You were taught, with regard to your former way of life, to put off your old self, which is being corrupted by its deceitful desires; to be made new in the attitude of your minds; and to put on the new self, created to be like God in true righteousness and holiness" (Eph. 4:22–24). Again, Paul encourages the church at Colosse to lift its eyes to Christ: "We proclaim him, admonishing and teaching everyone with all wisdom, so that we may present everyone perfect in Christ" (Col. 1:28).

At least for me, this comparative process has proven ironic. The more I approach the Light, the more I see the imperfections and blemishes in my life. As a young Christian, I was totally oblivious to some of my failings. Now, they stand out in bold relief, stark and accusing. That compass is more accurate than I want it to be!

How Am I Doing–Am I There Yet?

All of these facets of our faith journey raise the question of maturity. If discipleship is relative, how will I know when I am a mature Christian? Paul perceived the need for and the reality of Christian maturity as he told the church at Ephesus to strive "until we all reach unity in the faith and in the knowledge of the Son of God and become mature, attaining to the whole measure of the fullness of Christ" (Eph. 4:13). The result of that maturity, according to Paul, is that those loyal to Christ will not be confused or misled by the ways of this world: "Instead, speaking the truth in love, we will in all things grow up into him who is the Head, that is, Christ" (Eph. 4:15). Maturity wraps itself around a process that is—you guessed it—relative and ongoing. Even Paul, a spiritual giant, recognized his continuing need to grow. Writing to his beloved friend Timothy near the end of his life, Paul confesses that he still is nowhere close to the maturity he desires:

> Here is a trustworthy saying that deserves full acceptance: Christ Jesus came into the world to save sinners—of whom I am the worst. But for that very reason I was shown mercy so that in me, the worst of sinners, Christ Jesus might display his unlimited patience as an example for those who would believe on him and receive eternal life. (1 Tim. 1:15–16)

Even at the end of his faithful life, Paul saw how immature he still was. Again, so much for arrogance or self-righteousness!

Emerging Truth about My Discipleship

Exchanging a world in which I am at the center for a world in which God is at the center begins wherever I am called to take a step of faith. As we continue to understand what discipleship looks like, the following truths about its relative dimension encourage us even as we struggle to grow and mature:

- *Discipleship is a relative process.* No two Christians have had the same faith journey. The path I follow is unique to me and me alone.
- *Comparing our faithfulness to that of other believers is problematic.* If we compare ourselves to those who are younger in the faith, we can become arrogant. If we compare ourselves to those who are more mature, we can become discouraged.
- *Being a Christian does not make you better than someone else; it makes you better than you were.* As we compare ourselves with ourselves, we should see a transformation in our attitudes and actions over time.
- *Christ Jesus is the ultimate compass for charting our faithfulness.* We have a long way to go!

Congregational Discipleship

The relative nature of my discipleship journey also applies to the church community as a whole. Let's turn to Scripture to better understand this dimension of discipleship.

A Variety of Steps, But One Faith

The phrase "next step of faith" is one of my favorites. It reinforces both the ongoing and relative dimensions of discipleship. The faithful always have another step to take, a step that is also unique because no two churches or believers are at the same exact spot on the journey. Though the theme of these steps is always faithfulness, the characteristics are always unique, belonging solely to the person or body undertaking the journey. I have witnessed this reality at conferences at which the leaders of various congregations hear the same message and walk away with completely different action items. As we hear God's truth, it is only natural and appropriate to personalize and perceive it through the lens of our own distinct context. If those same leaders gathered together several years later and heard the same presentation, they would no doubt discern new and different steps of faith. That is exactly my point—our discipleship journey is relative. A quick review of the Scriptures reveals this very principle: different "next steps of faith" are appropriate for different groups at different times under different circumstances.

GEOGRAPHIC STEPS

The Old Testament describes God's people, the nation of Israel, as having next steps of faith that were often just that—geographic steps. God literally calls Abram, the father of Israel, to take steps of faith: "Leave your country, your people and your father's household and go to the land I will show you" (Gen. 12:1). He travels to a new and foreign land at which time he receives a promise: "Abram traveled through the land as far as the site of the great tree of Moreh at Shechem...The Lord appeared to Abram and said, 'To your offspring I will give this land'" (Gen. 12:6a,7a). But that does not end the traveling or next steps of faith. With the reality of an intense famine, Abram and his clan travel to Egypt to live (Gen. 12:10). In time, their next step is to leave and embark on a return trip. As the story of God's people unfolds, the literal steps of faith continue unabated. After landing in Egypt again, Israel—Abraham's descendants—receive the call to follow God's appointed leader, Moses, to take the necessary steps to leave the bondage of a foreign land. Crossing the Red Sea becomes a step of faith like never before—a great opportunity to witness God's provision, power, and compassion. They take new steps of faith as they are led through the wilderness, trusting in God for the daily needs of food and water.

Even as the Hebrew people slowly learn to walk in faith, they see that God expects new and different steps for them as they continue their journey. As a people, Israel is called to trust God and take steps into the promised land, even though the countryside is filled with foreigners who possess great military strength. Unable to take this step of faith, Israel endures a punishing existence for many years until a new generation is ready to enter the land by faith (Num. 14:29–34). Years later, as Joshua leads the way, the next steps take the faithful through the deep end of the pool again, namely, the Jordan River at flood stage!

QUIET STEPS

In the New Testament, we see that stepping out in faith sometimes requires that we begin by standing absolutely still. The initial step of faith for the early disciples was to be still! As Jesus departs to be with God, the instructions are clear: "Do not leave Jerusalem, but wait for the gift my Father promised, which you have heard me speak about. For John baptized with water, but in a few days you will be baptized with the Holy Spirit" (Acts 1:4b–5). Are there times today when congregations would be well served by a season of "waiting on the Lord"–listening rather than acting? Absolutely! How tempting it is to do something– anything!–before we purposely pause to receive the Spirit's guidance. The corporate discipline of silence and reflection is nowhere close to a popular initiative these days. "Doing God's bidding" tends to depend upon my ability to decide and execute a plan. This style of plunging right in is familiar, appealing, and downright commendable from the human perspective. Prayerful discernment tends to require me to seek the Holy One's perspective–an uncomfortable and awkward strategy.

LOUD STEPS

As the Spirit boldly arrives on the day of Pentecost (Acts 2), the disciples know that the waiting and listening are over. Their next step was clear: open their mouths and proclaim the Good News. As the story of Acts progresses, this mission to share Jesus' story is a primary next step theme. Even in the face of persecution and life-threatening circumstances, the followers of Christ–the early church–courageously stand up for the Risen King. Their message spreads across geographic, ethnic, gender, and economic boundaries. Paul's letters reinforce how his obedience to the Great Commission to go and make disciples took on many different forms and styles. Though common themes and teaching appear throughout his letters, Paul tailors his correspondence so that each congregation–or region in the case of shared letters–receives a message with distinctive emphasis and specific instructions. The steps of faith that God calls disciples to take vary greatly depending on circumstances. Sometimes God's people are literally called to step out and physically move. At other times, congregations discern the challenge to follow specific and sometimes scary instructions right where they are–to bloom where they are planted. Even others may be asked to take quiet steps or even loud steps. The reality is that congregational discipleship is relative. God's faith-building call to your congregation is undoubtedly very different from my own.

Two Distinct Messages

As highlighted in the prior chapter, Christ communicated directly with seven churches via a revelation given to the apostle John (Rev. 2–3). Though all are called to steps of faith, differences always exist. Let's examine the unique calls for the churches of Smyrna and Laodicea.

The letter to the church at Smyrna (Rev. 2:8–11) is affirming. This body of believers is on the right track, and Jesus does not suggest any needed changes other than to keep on keeping on in its walk of faith. This is somewhat surprising given the context of this city. Smyrna was a wealthy and prosperous town. However, the church located there suffered for its faith, enduring a history of persecution toward Christians. One would surmise that such a rough environment would squelch the spreading of the gospel. If the hostility of the pagan and Roman powers were not enough, the Jews with political clout also actively hindered the church's ministry. Through it all, the believers at Smyrna remained faithful. Jesus commends them: "I know your afflictions and your poverty–yet you are rich!" (Rev. 2:9a). Their "wealth" is measured in their degree of obedience and faith. A great example of the last being first!

In contrast stand Jesus' words in the Laodicean letter–ouch! This is a letter of reproach. He lets them have both barrels. The setting of this church was not nearly as difficult as that in Smyrna. Built at the juncture of two highly traveled highways, the city was a wealthy industrial community as well as a seat of government. Apparently, the combination of these factors, along with the church's leadership, produced a collective apathy that Jesus was unwilling to tolerate much longer. "So, because you are lukewarm–neither hot nor cold–I am about to spit you out of my mouth" (Rev. 3:16). The challenge was not persecution and hardship from without, but complacency from within. Like most of the other seven letters, Jesus calls this church to take a reverse step, namely repentance. "Those whom I love I rebuke and discipline. So be earnest, and repent" (Rev. 3:19).

The Question of Maturity

As noted earlier, Paul was eager for the people of God to grow into maturity. Even as he doles out praise for the believers at Ephesus for their readiness to progress, he chides the church at Corinth because it apparently lacks maturity: "Brothers, I could not address you as spiritual but as worldly–mere infants in Christ. I gave you milk, not solid food, for you were not yet ready for it. Indeed, you are still not ready" (1 Cor. 3:1–2). Paul's assessment of the Corinthians indicates that they should have been ready to take their next step of faith but were merely standing still. So how do we, as members of the current church, evaluate our progress? As you might guess by now, I think congregational maturity is also relative. Another look again at the Revelation letters should provide insights on this subject.

The church at Philadelphia must have been splendid in its relative faithfulness: "I know your deeds. See, I have placed before you an open door that no one can shut. I know that you have little strength, yet you have kept my word and have not denied my name" (3:8). In another affirming letter, Jesus praises and encourages these believers to keep going without mentioning any areas for improvement. Of particular interest is Jesus' acknowledgement that they are weak. Perhaps the Philadelphians knew they were nowhere near "attaining the whole measure of the fullness of Christ" (Eph. 4:13b), but that did not prevent them from earnestly desiring that fullness. Christ saw and commended their spark of desire. The lesson for us is clear. Just because your church may currently be small, weak, or new does not suggest a lack of faithfulness. Discipleship is a process. Some smaller, weaker congregations are more mature than some of the larger and seemingly stronger churches. The deciding factor? Maturity is relative to each body of Christ and its level of desire to take its own, unique next step of faith

Congregational spiritual maturity—like our own—is dynamic, not static. A church's faithfulness and growth can only be measured on a sliding scale that constantly shifts based on what it currently is, where it has been, and what God has called it to be. Thus, the question for congregations is not, "Have we arrived?" but, "What is our next step of faith?" Those churches that continue to take steps of faith renew themselves. They stay engaged to the Spirit's leading, bear lasting fruit, and remain spiritually mature. Those that do not tend to lose their spiritual vibrancy, increasingly fall short of God's expectations for them, and fail to exhibit a mature congregational faith based on obedience to Christ the king.

One Final Pitfall: The Tendency to Transplant, not Transform

A failure to appreciate the relative nature of discipleship can easily mean that churches tend to act on the inappropriate urge to copy others rather than undergo the transformational "next steps of faith" that discipleship requires. Don't get me wrong; I am truly convinced that churches can greatly benefit from the experience of other congregations. To that end, I often encourage church leaders to attend conferences that will allow them to see the breadth of what God is doing through other faith communities. At the same time, I issue this warning: in the process of comparing notes, seek to identify the principles that will actually work in your church setting and avoid merely copying, at all costs. In other words, as you review what works for other churches, be sure to *still* use the right compass for your congregation: that is, measure yourself against yourself and also measure yourself against the overall vision of *your* church and no one else's church!

Emerging Truth about Our Discipleship

Jesus seemed to enjoy hanging out at the temple. On one particular visit, He was sitting near the temple treasury to observe what folks were dropping in the offering plate (Lk. 21:1–4). He used the occasion to teach his disciples about His own theory of relativity. Comparing a widow's donation of two small coins to the much larger contributions of the wealthy, Jesus commends the humble, sincere gift that came from the poor woman's big heart. Even though she was "weak" financially, her spiritual maturity was evident in Jesus' eyes. In telling his followers that she "put in more than all the others" (v. 3), Jesus confirms that discipleship is not about total size but about total commitment. Worship attendance, aggregate budget, staff size, the breadth of educational ministries, and the regularity of mission trips are a few common barometers of church health, strength, and vibrancy. But are they really? It seems to me that a "widow's mite" church is what we are called to be—giving as much as we know of ourselves to as much as we know of God. Always growing. Always striving to exchange our world for God's by taking the next step of faith. Always seeking to move closer and closer to reflecting kingdom values, attitudes, and traits.

As we continue our own discovery process, the following principles will help guide our way as His servants:

- *Congregational discipleship is a relative process.* No two churches possess the same faith history. The path we have been collectively called to follow is unique and should reflect the distinctiveness of our surrounding community. Each of us needs to bloom where we are planted.
- *Being faithful does not make a congregation better than other churches; it only makes it better than it was.* As we compare ourselves with ourselves, we should see a transformation in our attitudes and actions over time.
- *Maturity in Christ is dynamic, and it constantly evolves with our ongoing growth in Christ.* Each year brings new and often more challenging steps of faith for a church in process.

- *Transformation, not merely transplantation, is the goal of any church serious about its commitment to Christ.* What works in other churches can work in yours only if you keep in mind your relative compass: that is, your own church's vision for exchanging worlds.

DISCUSSION QUESTIONS

Personal Discipleship

1. As you grew up, with whom did you tend to compare yourself? What conclusions did you draw from doing so?

2. What are the cultural influences that encourage us to compare ourselves to those around us?

3. Reflect upon how God has worked in your life over the years. Specifically, what was your life circumstance five years ago to the day, and what significant lessons have you learned in the interim?

4. If spiritual maturity is dynamic and relative to our own experience, how would you rate your current spiritual maturity on a scale of 1–10, with 10 being fully mature? Explain your answer.

5. Identify a recent step of faith that Christ has been inviting you to take.

Congregational Discipleship

1. Which Old Testament character most impresses you for his or her faithfulness? Explain your answer.

2. What is an example from your congregation's past in which a significant step of faith was taken? What happened as a result?

3. Read and review an old newsletter from your congregation—ideally 5 years old. What has changed for the better? What has remained stuck in neutral?

4. If spiritual maturity is dynamic and relative to our own experience, how would you rate your church's current spiritual maturity on a scale of 1–10, with 10 being fully mature? Explain your answer.

5. If Christ wrote a personal letter to your church, what step of faith would He encourage the congregation to make?

5

A Purposeful Process

A Clear Destination

> *"'Love the Lord your God with all your heart and with all your soul and with all your mind.' This is the first and greatest commandment. And the second is like it: 'Love your neighbor as yourself.'"*
>
> JESUS (Mt. 22:37–39)

Six words can summarize the entire Bible: *good news, bad news, good news.*

Good News (Genesis 1 and 2): God creates a wonderful world, perfectly designed, both beautiful and functional. The plants, animals, and elements coexist in a remarkable, self-sustaining ecosystem. Into this marvelous environment, God introduces humanity—created in the image of the Divine. This Garden—the kingdom of God in all its fullness—is heaven on earth.

Bad News (Genesis 3–11): In the midst of this enchanted reality, we humans become arrogant and self-centered. We conclude that we know what's best for us, better than our Maker does. Why live within God's world and guidelines for life when we can create our own? So we exchange a world in which God is at the center for a world in which we are at the center. (Reverse discipleship!) Instead of following God, we follow ourselves, led by our own whims and impulses. The result: alienation from our Creator and one another as well as separation from the home we were meant to inhabit in the Garden. The consequences—pain, toil, trouble, and death—make our decision very bad news indeed.

Good News: (Genesis 12–Revelation 22): Grieved but undaunted by our rebellion, God's intent to redeem the world unfolds. In spite of our actions and "while we were still sinners" (Rom. 5:8), our patient Parent initiates a plan to save us from destruction, to save us from ourselves. With the call of Abraham (Gen. 12:1–3), God works in and through covenant people, world events, circumstances, and even animals to set the stage for the ultimate solution to our problem of alienation: Jesus, His Son. In Christ, the prodigal peoples of the world can return home. In following Jesus, we discover the clear, well-worn path that leads back to the Garden.

Six words capture the truth that God is at work even today to accomplish a divine purpose. Knowing the end from the very beginning, our Creator stops at nothing to orchestrate important kingdom business: paving the way for disciples to let go of our world and embrace a God-centered one.

This chapter explores the third of the five dimensions of discipleship—its *purposeful* nature. We have already seen that discipleship is a lifelong process that is uniquely related to our personal history both individually and collectively. Now we see that it has a clear destination for both me and us: kingdom living. Let's look more closely and see how the process works for both the individual disciple and the discipled church.

Personal Discipleship

Billy's "Don't Sit Still" Jesus

December 31, 1979. At 11:30 p.m., I was celebrating New Year's Eve with 18,000 other Christians in Champaign, Illinois, at InterVarsity's Urbana Missions Conference. For half an hour, the crowd had been enthusiastically singing, led by a choir of 4,000. The spiritual power and energy had built to a fevered pitch when up to the microphone stepped Billy Graham. For the next 30 minutes, Dr. Graham lit a flame under that crowd—a flame so intense that fireworks were completely unnecessary to usher in the new year. Billy Graham's message was simple: *"Come!"* and, *"Go!"* Back and forth he intricately wove Jesus' two imperatives to (1) "come unto me" to reclaim our citizenship in the kingdom of God, and (2) "go unto the world" to use our spiritual gifts to change the world. Sewn together, they formed a web that caught the very purpose of our Christian walk:

"Come and you will see."
"Go now and leave your life of sin."
"Come, follow me."
"Go and proclaim the kingdom of God."
"Come with me by yourselves to a quiet place and get some rest."
"Go into all the world and preach the good news to all creation."
"Come to me and drink."
"Go! I am sending you out like lambs among wolves."

"Come to me, all you who are weary and burdened, and I will
    give you rest."
"Go and make disciples of all nations, baptizing them in the
    name of the Father and of the Son and of the Holy Spirit."

Over and over, he pounded these two little words into our souls:
come and *go, come* and *go, come* and *go*. How could these two small verbs
be packed with so much action, so much purpose? This dynamic sermon
is one of only a handful I have ever remembered for any length of time.
Most of us in attendance didn't even bother to walk out of the arena
afterward. We just floated on the wings of the Spirit's vitality and
inspiration. Dr. Graham's message that night was not original, but was
it ever clear and effective! All of us understood what our roles were
when we left. We were—and are—to "come," cultivating a process of
ongoing spiritual growth to promote Christ's redemptive work. We must
also "go," seizing daily opportunities to live out kingdom values within
our world.

Jesus' Old Testament Message on Purpose

Not surprisingly, Dr. Graham's twofold sermon was grounded in
the words of Jesus as exemplified by His encounter with an "expert in
the law." "Teacher, which is the greatest commandment in the Law?"
asked the Jewish man (Mt. 22:36). In other words, What is really
important? What is the ultimate purpose of my life? This so-called expert
was trying to throw Him a curve ball, but Jesus hit it over the fences like
a slow pitch tossed right down the middle. He homered a short and
sweet response, nothing more than a few key verses from the Old
Testament: "Love the LORD your God with all your heart and with all
your soul and with all your strength" (Deut. 6:5) and "...Love your
neighbor as yourself" (Lev. 19:18b). How simple and at the same time
complete! We are to allow God to be our God (come) and make a
difference in the lives of those around us (go).

On-the-Job Training

From Dr. Graham, I heard the recorded words of Christ come alive
and define purpose for me. The early followers of Christ, though, had no
gospels to turn to for guidance and direction. To remain focused, they
relied on the "apostles' teaching" (Acts 2:42), the ever-present guidance
of the Spirit, and their collective memory of the Master's teaching: "Love
God and love your neighbor," and "Come and go." History and the
letters of the New Testament confirm that indeed they lived out these
commands and faithfully stayed on track. Let's take a moment to learn
from their witness.

NEW CREATION

Paul repeatedly emphasizes our need to have a transformational relationship with Jesus Christ, the essence of loving God with our heart, mind, and soul. Our old and self-centric ways have no place in the kingdom and must be shed because they are ill-fitting. A complete change of clothing is required: "putting off" the tattered and filthy lifestyle that we are used to and "putting on" the attributes of Christ (Eph. 4:17ff, Col. 3:12ff). As you might suspect, new clothes have an entirely new feel. Paul calls for nothing less than life-changing transformation as he urges the church in Rome to don spiritual apparel:

> Therefore, I urge you, brothers, in view of God's mercy, to offer your bodies as living sacrifices, holy and pleasing to God—which is your spiritual worship. Do not conform any longer to the pattern of this world, but be transformed by the renewing of your mind. Then you will be able to test and approve what God's will is—his good, pleasing and perfect will. (Rom. 12:1–2)

So, how does transformation look as a garment? Paul states: "Therefore, if anyone is in Christ, he is a new creation; the old has gone, the new has come!" (2 Cor. 5:17) In addition, the new wardrobe increasingly reflects the heart and purpose of God for a disciple. Paul tells the church in Ephesus: "[P]ut on the new self, created to be like God in true righteousness and holiness" (Eph. 4:24).

NEW GIFTS

Paul's contribution to our understanding of "going"—loving our neighbor—is also immense. In no uncertain terms, he is clear that our faith is not to be lived in isolation. Rather, it is a group project designed to make a difference in the lives of fellow believers and the world. Paul insightfully describes our relationship to other believers as a living organism: "The body is a unit, though it is made up of many parts; and though all its parts are many, they form one body. So it is with Christ… Now you are the body of Christ, and each one of you is a part of it" (1 Cor. 12:12, 27). As a Christian, I am to relate to other disciples just as the parts of my body work together to nurture all of me. If this analogy is not clear enough, we need only to look at Paul's "one another" directives. From his perspective, we are to be nothing less than our brother's keeper as we:

Serve one another	Galatians 5:13
Accept one another	Romans 15:7
Forgive one another	Colossians 3:13
Greet one another	Romans 16:16

Bear one another's burdens	Galatians 6:2
Be devoted to one another	Romans 12:10
Honor one another	Romans 12:10
Teach one another	Romans 15:14
Submit to one another	Ephesians 5:21
Encourage one another	1 Thessalonians 5:11

Glancing through this list tells me that maintaining the Body of Christ can be *a lot* of work! But we are never left without the resources to function purposefully and contribute meaningfully to the Body's upkeep. As new Christians, we have new *spiritual* gifts (1 Cor. 12:11) and fruit (Gal. 5:5), which are intended to help us minister to others. (The root meaning of *minister* is "to serve.") Spiritual gifts are "divine abilities distributed by the Holy Spirit to all believers by God's design and grace for the common good of the Body of Christ."[1] In the same way that all humans are given natural talents at their physical birth, the Spirit bestows spiritual gifts to new disciples at their spiritual birth. When understood in the context of their passions to serve in a particular area, their unique personalities, and their life commitments, disciples can discover where they are most effective and fulfilled in service.

Paul well understood the importance of appreciating and using the spiritual gifts bestowed on us. In his letters to the Corinthians, Ephesians, and Romans, he expounds on this concept of spiritual gifts with clarity. "Now about spiritual gifts, brothers, I do not want you to be ignorant… There are different kinds of gifts, but the same Spirit. There are different kinds of service, but the same Lord. There are different kinds of working, but the same God works all of them in all men"(1 Cor. 12:1,4–6; see also Rom. 12, Eph. 4, and 1 Pet. 4).

Emerging Truth about My Discipleship

The process of exchanging my world for God's has a clear, purposeful objective: to allow me to experience God's love (coming) and, in turn, make a unique contribution to building the kingdom (going). As we continue to understand what discipleship looks like, the following truths about its purposeful dimension encourage us even as we take our next step of faith.

- *Discipleship is a purposeful process.* Our journey has a kingdom of God destination.
- *Reaching our destination involves a twofold process:* coming and going; loving God and loving our neighbor; being and doing. A transformational relationship with Jesus Christ empowering us to then make a difference in the world around us.

- *Each believer is a unique servant.* Our spiritual gifts—combined with our passions, personality, and life experiences—guide us to effective and fulfilling service.

As Graham so simply stated, coming and going are the activities that are our true purpose. As disciples, we are called to be in balance, like a bird with two powerfully spread wings working in sync. Only then will our flight be effective; only then will our flight lead us home.

Congregational Discipleship

God's Destination and Purpose for His Church

Though the *process* of God's workings is at times challenging to anticipate (Eph. 3:4–6), the *content* of the Holy One's purpose is crystal clear. Our Parent's objective is for us to find the path that leads us to our ultimate destination and then to proceed to this kingdom home designed just for us. Collectively as the Church of Jesus Christ, we are to help as many people as possible go home.

THE GARDEN: GOD'S BEST

The ultimate destination for God's people is beautifully captured in the first two chapters of Genesis. Home sweet home. Paradise. The kingdom of God on earth. Eden was indeed a perfect setting for our existence, designed just for you and me with the provisions of nature, the partnership of others, and the presence of God. Our God's intent covers the bases for our most basic needs: we are loved beyond measure, we are able to accept and extend love to our fellow humans, and we are purposeful as we use our gifts to tend to "garden" chores. God's highest hope was that the created people would enjoy being in community with their Creator, one another, and the creation forever. This is still God's objective; nothing has changed. The Holy One desires that you and I be citizens of the kingdom and take hold of all the privileges therein. But the original path to this destination has clearly been thwarted by our choice to put ourselves instead of God at the center of our existence (Gen. 3–11). Fortunately for our sake, He knew that we would make this choice beforehand. For that reason, the Lamb (Jesus) was chosen before the foundation of the world (1 Pet. 1:17–21).

GOD'S RESPONSE IS REVEALED: RESTORATION

God is sovereign. In spite of our noncooperation, the Creator continues to work to achieve kingdom ends. Genesis 3–11 details the awful after-effects of our choosing to elevate ourselves over our Creator instead of heeding God's call and prescription for obedience and healthy living spelled out in Genesis 1 and 2. A holy and just God cannot tolerate our rebellion, and we are banished from the Garden. Let's examine the depth of this consequence. Outside of the Garden, the landscape is drastically different: God's children, made in the divine image, are now trapped as prisoners and slaves, ruled over by the Evil One, the prince of the world. Does this disastrous turn of events discourage or destroy God's ambitions and dreams? Not on your life! God loves the Garden. The Creator made it just for us and yearns for us to enjoy it. God is intent on solving the big problem—sin and its consequences—we humans have created.

God's solution to the problem of sin begins with the call of Abraham (Gen. 12) and is fulfilled through Jesus, whose name means "salvation." What an apt description, given His destiny. Through His sacrificial life, death, and resurrection, we, the captives of the prince of this world, gained an avenue of escape from the consequences of sin. God exchanged Jesus' life as a timely ransom, buying us back—literally "redeeming" us—to fulfill the original plan. Disciples—those of us who acknowledge that redemption by exchanging a self-centered world for a Christ-centered world—blessedly discover the path back to the garden. We can finally go home.

The Role of the Church: Sustaining the Restoration Process

Jesus had great vision and hope for how the Church would fit into this history of salvation and God's active work in the world. As evidenced by Jesus' Great Commission (Mt. 28:19–20) and His comments just before His ascension, the community of faith has an extraordinarily important role: "But you will receive power when the Holy Spirit comes on you; and you will be my witnesses in Jerusalem, and in all Judea and Samaria, and to the ends of the earth" (Acts 1:8). We are, therefore, to continue the work He has started with His twofold strategy: (1) proclaim His *message* of hope—the content of the Good News and the plan of salvation, and (2) do so by utilizing His *method* of kingdom building—the process of making disciples who make disciples.

Unfortunately, in both my consulting practice and congregational roles, I typically find that congregational leaders and pastors turn to the Bible for the "message," but not the "method." They are usually able to articulate the essentials of the Gospel with relative ease, but they then adopt secular models of leadership rather than Jesus' empowering "method"—the process of mobilizing disciples. (I will address the reasons for this more fully in the next chapter.) In seeking to address this shortcoming in understanding, I often summarize Jesus' method in an easy to remember trilogy of words: *invite, grow,* and *send.*

THE BASICS OF JESUS' METHOD

In my mind, Jesus was the first church pastor, and His methodology is a self-evident truth. First, He set out to establish a community of faith by proclaiming the Good News: Himself! He extended an invitation to learn about the kingdom and spoke, lived, and exemplified its values. Many who heard Him followed to become part of this new movement. Next, He chose His key disciples–"apostles"–as the recipients of His customized, empowering training. Even though He taught, guided, and nurtured all who desired to grow spiritually, He invested focused time and mentored the twelve who would provide the critical future leadership for this movement of God. Finally as the end of His time on earth approached, Jesus began to hand over the leadership reins to this carefully groomed band of committed followers. The fruit of His empowering efforts showed itself at Pentecost as His commissioned emissaries spread the Good News first embodied in their fearless Leader. Three sequential steps: Jesus *invited* His listeners to follow, *grew* those whose hearts were open and receptive, and *sent* His prepared disciple-making disciples into the world. Jesus raised up the first disciple-making disciples, and here we are, two thousand years later, the beneficiaries of His brilliant pastoring.[2]

PAUL'S CHURCH PLANTING PROCESS

Paul, also a student of Christ, was an excellent imitator of the Master Teacher's method. Paul's first step in making disciples who make disciples was *inviting* his listeners to take their next step of faith–ministry by multiplication, not just addition. For many, that step was their first. His proclamation of the Good News predictably identified those who were enthusiastic and who would become the core of a new congregation. Once a nucleus of committed converts was formed, Paul moved on to the second step: *growing* followers of Christ, which he did through subsequent visits and letters to encourage the faithful. Paul's third step– *sending*–empowered believers and ministry teams to be ambassadors for Christ. Along the way, he enabled them to understand their spiritual gifts, passions, and spheres of influence. Paul trained the faithful and then commissioned them by leaving the local ministry in their capable hands. The best New Testament example of this discipling model is the church at Ephesus. Paul invested himself heavily in the formation and development of this congregation. His letter to this community represents the best picture of how the body of believers is to function effectively. Paul clearly lays out the heart of the method of Christ's Church:

> It was he [Christ] who gave some to be apostles, some to be prophets, some to be evangelists, and some to be pastors and

teachers, to prepare God's people for works of service, so that the body of Christ may be built up until we all reach unity in the faith and in the knowledge of the Son of God and become mature, attaining to the whole measure of the fullness of Christ. (Eph. 4:11–13, author's emphasis)

Paul understood that the Church's role was not only to proclaim the Gospel hope, but to birth, cultivate, and mobilize disciples. Believers with specific spiritual gifts and hearts for investing their lives in others (4:11) would prepare willing servants who would then go on to prepare still others—making disciples who make disciples (4:12). Note the key verb *"prepare"* in this passage. This term translates the Greek word *kataristmon,* which connotes images of setting a broken bone, mending a frayed net, furnishing an empty house, restoring to mint condition, or training an athlete. Paul's selection of this term is compelling because it conveys an essential truth: Jesus' method is a highly intentional process.

TODAY'S MAJOR OBSTACLE: HIRE, WATCH, PAY

Throughout this book, I have been defining discipleship as a process of exchange—letting go of our agenda and embracing God's. I have also depicted discipleship as an ongoing process involving a path that connects the two ends of a continuum, represented by the kingdom of the world on one end and the kingdom of God on the other. Disciples are those sojourners who have turned from the former and are proceeding home as kingdom citizens. An important question to ask regarding this issue of methodology is this: if congregational discipleship means increasingly *embracing* Jesus' method of invite…grow…send, then what should we be *letting go of?* My immediate answer is "hire…watch…pay"—*hiring* pastors and staff to get ministry accomplished, *watching* them do their job, and *paying* them for their time. (Bill Easum calls this model "pastor fetch"— throwing the heavy bulk of work to the hired professionals; cajoling them to pick it up and run; and congratulating them when, exhausted, they drop the completed ministry agenda at our feet. What a descriptive image!) What else would you expect in our Western world, where money is more plentiful than time, and convenience is more appealing than sweat?

But hire…watch…pay is not God's design for the church. It is really nothing more than a strategy to secure a caretaker or chaplain who will serve the needs of consumeristic club members without involving the commitment of those in the club. It is a model that reeks of self-centeredness. In sharp contrast, invite…grow…send is a strategy to mobilize disciples to meet the needs of a hurting world. It is a method that requires crucifixion, both personal and corporate, so that the Great Commission can be fulfilled in loving obedience to Christ the King.

Emerging Truth about Our Discipleship

The purpose of the Church is not a complex matter: proclaim the Good News, nurture and prepare those who respond, and mobilize them to share their new hope using a relational, face-on-face methodology. Bill Hull uses several metaphors to capture this truth. He claims the Church is called to

- act as a *hospital* that invites the sick and hurting to have their needs met
- construct *greenhouses* that incubate and grow fruit-bearing believers
- set up *training centers* that send strong, equipped disciples into the world to make disciples[3]

The bottom line is this: the local church is to help as many people as possible to go home, emulating Jesus' method of empowering growing disciples to be and to do, to come and to go, to love God and to love their neighbors. That's the realization of the Great Commission. That's the fulfillment of Jesus' vision, which He cast to His committed followers (Acts 1:8). Ultimately, that's the model that Jesus Himself demonstrated for us.[4] We ignore it at our own self-defeating risk.

As we continue to understand what discipleship together looks like, the following truths about its purposeful dimension encourage us even as we take our next step of faith.

- *Congregational discipleship has a clear destination.* Our journey together has a divine purpose—to pave the way for God's people to return to the Garden, God's kingdom.
- *Living out the Church's Great Commission requires personal and corporate crucifixion.* A self-serving model of church life—hire…watch…pay— is not the path to spiritual vitality and not that for which Christ gave His life.
- *Fulfilling our purpose involves a twofold strategy.* We are to collectively proclaim God's Good News ("*the message*") and implement a biblically based system ("*the method*") that *invites* the hurting to discover spiritual health, *grows* those whose lives are being transformed, and *sends* those who have been prepared to share the Good News.

Discipleship is never easy. The path can seem full of uncertainty and fear. But if I can hold before me the ultimate purpose of my life—to return home and bring as many with me as I can—then, with the promised help of the Holy Spirit (Jn. 14:16, Acts 1:8), I can focus on my next deliberate step of faith. So, too, can the Church of Jesus Christ.

DISCUSSION QUESTIONS

Personal Discipleship

1. Which of the two great commandments—love God and love your neighbor—do you find easier to fulfill? Explain your response.

2. What are the contemporary obstacles that Christians face in living a life that is focused on godly purposes? Which of them is most challenging for you?

3. When you review the "one another" list on pages 56–57, which one of them do you find yourself most easily fulfilling? Why is that?

4. In what service-related activity have you felt most effective and fulfilled? What was it about this opportunity that made it so rewarding?

5. Read Romans 12:6–8; Ephesians 4:11–13; 1 Corinthians 12:27–31. Based on your experience and understanding, which of the spiritual gifts listed best describes your passion for ministry?

Congregational Discipleship

1. Read Genesis 1–2. What appeals to most about the ideal world that God created?

2. Which aspect of Paul's three-part strategy—*invite, grow,* or *send*—is your congregation most fully accomplishing? Why and how?

3. Which aspect of Paul's three-part strategy—*invite, grow,* or *send*—is your congregation fulfilling the least? Why is that?

4. What are the obstacles that your church would have to overcome to more fully realize its calling in the dimension identified in question 3?

5. If "hire...watch...pay" is a 1 and "invite...grow...send" is a 10, locate your church's current mind-set. Explain your answer.

6

A Contentious Process

Divided Loyalties

I have fought the good fight, I have finished the race, I have kept the faith.

PAUL (2 Tim. 4:7)

Join me as I listen in on a one-way conversation, a little girl talking to herself: "This yellow brick road is great—I think. I have made some new friends—strange, but nice—to help along the way. They're called the Tin Man, the Lion, and the Scarecrow. As we skip down the road, we sing songs and see some cute Munchkins. We also get a little scared—well, maybe more than a little! Maybe some people would like this adventure, but I just want to go back to the home I am used to!"

Sound familiar? The sentiments of Dorothy in *The Wizard of Oz* hit pretty close to the mark for most Christians, who at times grow tired of plodding along on what seems to be an endless path. Not only is the walking hard, but the potholes of inner struggles and the nasty overgrowth of temptations can make the journey of faith downright unpleasant. Like Dorothy, we, too, want to go home.

And there's the rub: *which* home do we long for? The reality is that we have two homes: one to abandon and another to occupy. As I have been emphasizing all along, Jesus has invited us to leave our worldly home where we are kings and queens and travel to a new kingdom residence where God reigns supreme. But this ongoing process of saying good-bye to our self-centered values is tough. After all, we have grown used to a "natural" habitat—the way of this world—that has surrounded us from birth. To further confuse our move, in this life we cannot fully visualize the new home that Jesus offers. As we just saw, the difficulty of driving our spiritual U-Haul on an uncertain "yellow brick road" can make us homesick for our old digs.[1]

The local church is not immune to this struggle, either. Many congregations also feel this tension and struggle because their identities are confused by partial loyalty to *multiple* cultures–or homes. Predictably, they can become splintered as factions within a church struggle for control. This type of turmoil closely parallels the experience of the individual believer, with one major difference: In the church, the tension is much more externalized. I feel the invisible tug of war inside of me, but the local church sees the visible struggle right before its very eyes.

This chapter explores the fourth of the five dimensions of discipleship–its *contentious* nature. We have already seen that discipleship is an ongoing process that is uniquely related to our personal history and specific talents. Each of these dimensions helps us more clearly see and move toward our ultimate kingdom destination. Now, we will explore the inevitable battle scars that we acquire along the way as we uneasily struggle between a culture that focuses on self and a culture that focuses on God. Like oil and water, the two cultures do not mix, no matter how hard we try to put the two together. The only predictable result? Tension! No matter how earnestly we desire to be faithful followers of Christ, we quickly see that the Bible portrays discipleship as a process that is inherently and fundamentally conflicted. Let's see how the process works for both the individual disciple and the discipled church.

Personal Discipleship

Stubborn as a...

From time to time, I have joked about wanting to birth a new parachurch ministry called *Donkeys for Christ.* My intent has never been to make fun of any ministry, but to start a Christian organization where I am a model member! Why? I know I can be positively mule-ish in my own faith journey, becoming downright, self-servingly stubborn by refusing to cooperate with God's work in my life. At such times, I go through a lot of inner turmoil and distress. I know what I should do, but I won't do it. Oh, I eventually give in, but usually not before a knock down, drag out wrestling match with God. I kick, scream, and bray; and my Heavenly Parent patiently waits for me to give up and give in. As I scan the pages of the Scriptures, I see other contentious disciples as well. I suppose some could even qualify as patron saints of my new ministry!

DAVID'S BLATANT DISOBEDIENCE

How about King David? Of all the Old Testament figures, David stands out as one of the–if not *the*–most Spirit-filled followers of God. He is the only one described as enjoying the ongoing presence of God's

Spirit: "So Samuel took the horn of oil and anointed him [David] in the presence of his brothers, and from that day on the Spirit of the LORD came upon David in power" (1 Sam. 16:13). Indeed, the many psalms–literally songs–that David wrote reveal a man who was truly dedicated to, and desirous of, God's best (Ps. 27:4). One of David's psalms details David's internal struggle as the result of an incident in which even he–for a time–stubbornly refused to acknowledge his sin. Here's the backdrop: While standing on the roof of his palace one day, David spotted a beautiful woman–Bathsheba–and decided to use his kingly powers to indulge his sexual appetite (2 Sam. 11 and 12). After Bathsheba became pregnant, David went to great lengths to cover his tracks, ultimately causing her husband to be killed as David attempted to avoid detection and escape the consequences. During Bathsheba's pregnancy, David ran from God and failed to acknowledge his multiple acts of blatant disobedience. His business-as-usual attitude, though, was nothing more than a charade, for his sin was clear to many around him. Caught like a deer (or maybe a mule!) in the headlights by the prophet Nathan, David admitted the error of his ways. His subsequent writing of Psalm 32 tells us a great deal about the inner turmoil and contention he felt during this period of time (vv. 3–5).

A NEW TESTAMENT INDUCTEE

Within the pages of the New Testament, Paul also has the markings of a contentious saint. Don't misinterpret my tongue-in-cheek remarks. Paul was a great servant of Christ and is worthy of the highest praise. He is unquestionably honored as one of the finest servants to have ever walked with God. But he was also very human, and his own transparent writings reveal the depth of his daily struggle to be faithful. Understanding that discipleship is an ongoing battle, Paul encourages one of his standout pupils, Timothy, to not give up: "Fight the good fight of the faith. Take hold of the eternal life to which you were called when you made your good confession in the presence of many witnesses" (1 Tim. 6:12). At the end of his life, Paul acknowledges to Timothy that he himself has been engaged in the same struggle: "I have fought the good fight, I have finished the race, I have kept the faith" (2 Tim. 4:7). Internal conflict was a reality for Paul that spanned his entire Christian experience, from his road to Damascus calling until his death.

In his letter to the Romans, Paul explains that all disciples are inherently conflicted between what Paul calls our "sinful nature" or "old self" and the Spirit's ongoing, redemptive work in our minds: "So then, I myself in my mind am a slave to God's law, but in the sinful nature a slave to the law of sin" (Rom. 7:25). We are spiritually bipolar: our sinful nature is self-centered, while our redeemed minds are God-centered. In complete candor, Paul reveals the depth of his struggle to be faithful: "I do not understand what I do. For what I want to do I do not do, but what I hate I do…As it is, it is no longer I myself who do it, but it is sin living in me…For I have the desire to do what is good, but I cannot carry it out" (Rom. 7:15, 17, 18b). When I read these words, I think, "If Paul felt this way, there's hope for me!" Realistically, all disciples are candidates to be participants in my new "donkey" ministry. We all know the struggle involved in seeking to exchange a world in which we are at the center for a world in which God is at the center. I, for one, sincerely wish it were not such a battle. I would much prefer that discipleship be as instantaneous as I described earlier. Find me the magic wand. Tell me about the Web site where I can click on an "instantaneous" button and avoid the daily, ongoing war that wages within me.

Here's the bottom line: the redemptive work of God in our hearts has begun, but is not finished. The power of sin has been broken in the life of the believer—sin no longer reigns, but still remains. A part of our old self is still fond of what the world offers, while another, spiritual part longs to grow deeper in Christ and know the power of His resurrection. We are caught between two worlds, two sets of competing values, with each one vying to be our first love. So, the push and pull for our affections, allegiances, and, yes, our very souls is contentious to the very core.

The Struggle from Without

Do you read the comics? One character, Pogo, said it all for me: "We have met the enemy and he is us." The greatest struggle and contention that I experience on my discipleship journey occurs within me. The kingdoms of my world and God's world uncomfortably coexist, each vying for supremacy of my mind and body. I despise having my feet planted here even as my heart wants to go home. I would be remiss, however, if I did not also mention the contention that we often feel as Christians living and working in an ungodly world. Why, even our families, workplaces, and neighborhoods can—and often do—serve as springboards of opposition to the kingdom values we struggle to uphold. Does that surprise you? It shouldn't. Remaining faithful in the midst of an opposing culture is challenging for all disciples. Remember that pesky ongoing dimension of discipleship? Finally, let me acknowledge the brave followers of Christ for whom the battle is a life and death struggle. Those who travel the world can plainly witness to the spiritual warfare waged by faithful Christians as they are threatened with physical harm. For some, the main struggle is counting the cost of discipleship and being willing to bear the brunt of that cost, a cost that has death staring them in the face each day.

Whether our greatest assault is from within or around us, Paul's admonition to the Ephesians is wise and sobering advice: "Finally, be strong in the Lord and in his mighty power. Put on the full armor of God so that you can take your stand against the devil's schemes" (Eph. 6:10–11). These words are a call to arms. Our battles will be more than we can handle on our own. We will *never* be strong enough to defeat the power of evil, no matter what shape it takes or what time it comes knocking at our particular door. Our God knows the attacks we must endure before we can declare victory and go home. Let's be quick to don the armor that the Holy One has already designed for us.

Emerging Truth about My Discipleship

One of our greatest challenges as disciples is that we are trapped smack in the middle of two realities, firmly caught in an ongoing tug of war. Still living daily in this world and being drawn by its influences and allure, we are also gradually becoming citizens of God's world. In the midst of this relentless contention, we hear the blessed invitation of a grace-filled Savior, "Come to me, all you who are weary and burdened, and I will give you rest. Take my yoke upon you and learn from me…and you will find rest for your souls" (Mt. 11:28–29). These words of Jesus are demanding: we must exchange the "yoke" of our world for a Kingdom yoke. For all disciples, this process is contentious.

As we continue to journey on an oftentimes difficult road of faith, the following principles will help guide us:

- *Discipleship is a contentious process.* We cannot escape the conflict—ever.
- *The struggle stems from the clash of competing values.* We are caught between two opposite worlds, one that is self-serving, while the other is God-honoring. Sometimes the fiercest battles are inside our own souls, while at other times, they are external and all around us.

Congregational Discipleship

Two Against Ten

By now you should have a sneaking suspicion that the Scriptures are full of stories in which contention takes center stage, not only for individuals but for entire communities of faith. To test this theory out, take your Bible, open it up at random, and put your finger on a verse—any verse! Now, scan forward and backward in the Holy Book until you find a rather unholy, donkey-like element surfacing. It can take the form of creation at odds with God, God in a battle with the evil one, or human pitted against human. You haven't gone far in either direction, have you?

Today, I landed at Numbers 13, a story of Israel's divided loyalty. Moses—empowered by God's Spirit—has led the people of Israel out of Egypt, and they have traveled to the edge of Canaan, the promised land. The Lord speaks to Moses and communicates several clear messages: "Send some men to explore the land of Canaan, which I am giving to the Israelites. From each ancestral tribe send one of its leaders" (v. 1). This field trip serves two purposes. *First,* God wants a representative handful of leaders to do some recognizance. God knows what it looks like, but the people need to hear of its beauty and provision from their own peers. *Second,* God intends to reinforce a prior message—by divine authority, the land will belong to this community of faith. So Moses rounds up twelve leaders, details the instructions to gather strategic information, and sends them off.

Unfortunately, the eyesight—or should I say insights—of the twelve spies varies greatly depending on who's doing the observing. Ten of the spies see the land wearing lenses tinted with their own worldly and self-centric perspective. They see all the good things and agree that the territory looks wonderful. But their focus is on the big bad guys already living in Canaan who appear strong and scary. "We went into the land to which you sent us, and it does flow with milk and honey! Here is its fruit. But the people who live there are powerful, and the cities are fortified and very large" (vv. 27–28a). The other two spies, however, have a completely different perspective. Joshua and Caleb see and evaluate Canaan through lenses tinted with God's grace and sovereign power. Obviously, their report contradicts and challenges the one already shared. "Then Caleb silenced the people before Moses and said, 'We should go up and take possession of the land, for we can certainly do it'" (v. 30). Does it seem as if these two are talking about a whole different parcel of land than the other ten? Their lenses put a spiritual hue on the very physical reality before them. That evening, an internal struggle flares as people pick sides and verbally spar over what to do. Most folks, choosing to look through the same fear-inducing lenses as the ten spies, are convinced that danger and impossibility will surround their efforts to take the land. Once again it is the "Back to Egypt Committee" speaking:

> All the Israelites grumbled against Moses and Aaron, and the whole assembly said to them, "If only we had died in Egypt! Or in this desert! Why is the LORD bringing us to this land only to let us fall by the sword? Our wives and children will be taken as plunder. Wouldn't it be better for us to go back to Egypt?" And they said to each other, "We should choose a leader and go back to Egypt." (14:2–4)

In the clear minority are those who choose to see the conquest through the lenses tinted with kingdom values where God is God, period. Understanding the consequences of the nation's collective doubt and disobedience, Joshua and Caleb tear their clothes and forcefully speak their minds. "The land we passed through and explored is exceedingly good. If the LORD is pleased with us, he will lead us into that land, a land flowing with milk and honey, and will give it to us. Only do not rebel against the LORD. And do not be afraid of the people of the land, because we will swallow them up. Their protection is gone, but the Lord is with us. Do not be afraid of them" (14:7b-9).

This story shows us contentiousness on two different levels. First, we see a symptomatic element whereby two different groups vary in their opinions about the best plan of action. Based on the data available, they arrive at opposite conclusions. The result? Deep disagreement occurs as some think that proceeding into Canaan is foolish, while others consider it an opportunity. On a deeper level, though, the superficial issue—whether or not to enter the land—reveals a systemic difference in *core values,* whereby the two groups embrace antithetical cultures. What is important to the Joshua and Caleb group—the Lordship of the Creator—is clearly of minimal importance to the other group. For the faithful people, trusting in God and His ability to deliver on His promises is the preeminent value to embrace. In spite of any fears, their dependence on God is more important than their limited human perspective.

In contrast, the most important value for the majority is trust in self. Predictably, their fears incapacitate them. Again, faithful discipleship is exchanging a world in which our own perspective is primary for a world in which God's perspective is primary. In this case, the people were not able to complete this exchange and walk by faith. Their consequences were dire as they turned back from the promised land and spent many years walking in the desert instead.

Today's Traditional Version

In my teaching, I try to make complex matters understandable; and I hope that by this juncture of your reading, you are benefiting from my style. Hyperbole is a time-tested communication strategy and one of my favorites. So bear with me as I use this approach to make a point about the reality of many churches today. At the end of the last chapter, I highlighted Jesus and Paul's three-step method for church development—invite…grow…send—as one way to understand the purpose of the Church. I linked this biblical pattern to Bill Hull's metaphors of a hospital (inviting the sick), a greenhouse (nurturing the faithful as they bud and grow), and a training center (sending mature disciples into the community and the world) as an effective way to define faithful church life. In contrast, I pointed out that many local churches have regrettably fallen prey to the polar opposite–hire...watch...pay. The clashes of core values shown in these two church paradigms, and what those clashes imply, are of enormous importance.

Fully realized, invite...grow...send is the exact image of the ideal kingdom-focused church. This framework frees a church to proclaim a culturally relevant Gospel message through large settings like worship, as well as through skilled, individualized discipling opportunities. It lets a church grow members in their faith by emphasizing spiritual disciplines that include relationship-building, caring, learning, and serving. Finally, this model empowers trained and equipped disciples to serve in the kingdom hospitals, greenhouses, or training centers, depending upon their spiritual gifts, personalities, and passions. A church that embraces invite...grow...send proclaims its love through willing obedience to Christ's teachings. This kind of community agrees with Christ that its mission is to make disciples of all nations. Therefore, members would rightfully expect the pastor to act as a trainer, actively coaching them to use their spiritual gifts for the building of Christ's kingdom. This church is on fire and alive. This church is a monarchy where Christ is King.

Just the opposite of invite...grow...send is a typical, traditional version, namely *hire...watch...pay.* This model smacks of a club mentality because it represents a gathering of folks organized around its own members' consumeristic needs. This kind of congregation partially resembles the greenhouse I referred to earlier. Why? The core values of this kind of community are to take care of those within its walls. These church folks are not interested in acting as a hospital to those who need real spiritual healing. After all, why would they want to be around all those "sick" people? Even if they become healthy, these newcomers could change the way things are done, possibly ruining the club. Also, would a hire...watch...pay church be likely to turn into a training center? Definitely not! The core values of this church reinforce the status quo. Why rock the boat by becoming a place where members are challenged to use their gifts to bring even more "sick" people into the church?

The image of a greenhouse, however, has a lot of appeal. In such a setting, the members expect the pastor to act as a chaplain, a caretaker, or a greenhouse worker. In that role, the pastor can water, fertilize, and gently help the congregation to grow within its own cozy incubator. In this setting, church members highly value fellowship with one another in a nurturing, nonthreatening environment. This kind of congregation is really not a church at all; it's a club in which people *decide* on what they want instead of *discerning* what God wants. For this group, the one foundational core value on which all other values are based is love of self and of others who fit the mold. Christ is not King, but merely a respected peer.

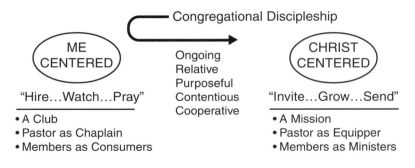

Am I painting too stark a picture? Yes, and frankly, I have never encountered a church that totally fit either the invite...grow...send or the hire...watch...pay paradigm. That is exactly my point. As a disciple, I am a combination of two competing cultures–the kingdom of the world, the origin of my natural birth, and the kingdom of God, into which I have been born again. I am spiritually bipolar, just like Paul describes himself. At times, my spiritual walk makes a pit stop at "Burger King" where I have it my way. At other times, I stand aside and acknowledge Christ as King and bow to his way. Why should we expect the local church, which is a community of double-minded disciples, to be any different?

A Double-Minded Church

Just as you and I might describe ourselves as "spiritually bipolar," the Church needs to understand that it, too, has distinct, competing cultures that vie for dominance. Let me suggest that this collective reality be called what it is: *bicultural*.[2] Of course, some congregations have multiple cultures in terms of nationalities, ethnic backgrounds, or any other socioeconomic dimensions. Let me also add that any group can experience contention, which doesn't necessarily stem from spiritual conflict. For the purposes of this book, though, when I use the term *bicultural*, I am thinking of two antithetical spiritual cultures, namely invite...grow...send and hire...watch...pay.

Symptoms of Core Values Disagreements

By now, you may be wondering what all of this has to do with your own church. If you doubt that your congregation is comprised of these two cultures, let me suggest a few strategies to test your theory. Gather a good-sized cross section of church members and ask them to give you some feedback on some new ideas. After greetings and refreshments, start with an innocuous warm-up question: *What do you think of painting the sanctuary a new color to make it more inviting to the public?* Or how about this: *What do you think of starting our Sunday services one hour earlier so the time will be more attractive to outsiders?* If these initial inquiries don't reveal the existence of differing values, pick up the pace: *What do you think of our pastor training a team of lay caregivers so that the pastor does hospital visitations only on rare occasions?* Oh, and don't forget this zinger: *What do you think of changing our music style so that it is more appealing to the unchurched people of our community?* If at this point any doubt remains, lob the question that Bill Hybels posed to his congregation as mentioned in chapter 2: *What do you think about moving the Sunday worship services to mid-week so we can dedicate our weekend efforts to reaching the lost?*

Don't be confused by my questions. I am not suggesting that your church initiate any of these changes. Notice that all the feelers begin with an innocent-sounding "What do you think?" By merely testing the waters, you may find that, like the twelve spies described in the book of Numbers, your congregation is made of some people whose lenses are more tinted by hire…watch…pay, while others tend toward an invite…grow…send perspective. Eliciting what your members think about *symptomatic* changes will give you valuable information about which *core values* they currently prioritize. Here's the point: the continuum between hire…watch…pay and invite…grow…send is a long one. It is the same one described in chapter 1 between the kingdom of the world and the kingdom of God. The first paradigm is centered around me or us, and the latter is centered around Christ and His mission. Undoubtedly, the good folks in your congregation are aligned, grouped, and spread across the continuum from one end to the other.

Congregational discipleship is the process of letting go of hire…watch…pay and embracing invite…grow…send. It is the radical transformation of values: letting go of the self-serving, cozy club and reaching for a world in which Christ is King and in which His teachings are the cornerstones of our lives together as His Church. Along the path to spiritual growth and maturity, a congregation must be ready for contention to rear its head, just as in our individual journey of faith. More than anything, though, congregational discipleship is a spiritual process that repeatedly tests a church's core values. As always, the ultimate question to grapple with is simply this: *Who is in charge*?

Emerging Truth about Our Discipleship

Like individual disciples, churches find themselves caught in between two homes, or cultures: One culture reflects a worldly, self-centered bias, while the other takes on kingdom, Christ-centered priorities. When a congregation tends toward self-centeredness, it uses its energy to make its own members comfortable by providing for their own needs over and above any other. In so doing, the congregation begins to resemble a club—with hands molded in a permanent "insider's" handshake. When a congregation tends toward Christ-centeredness, it uses its energy to serve and transform the world, whether around the corner or around the globe. This type of church becomes a beacon—with hands extended in a permanent invitation to others. To some degree, all congregations are bicultural and reflect both of these bents. Faithful congregations, though, focus on increasingly turning their backs on the culture of the world and embracing the King's kingdom culture—this process is congregational discipleship.

Let's review the principles that by now are hopefully clear to us:

- *Discipleship is a contentious process.* We cannot escape the conflict—ever.
- *The struggle stems from the clash of competing values.* In God's Church, we are caught between two opposite worlds. One is self-serving (hire…watch…pay), while the other is God-honoring (invite…grow…send).
- *All churches are bicultural to some degree.* Churches reflect the bipolar nature that resides spiritually in each of us. The challenge is to take our next step of faith—moving further away from a world in which we are kings and queens, and closer to a world in which Christ is King.

By now, I know I must sound like a broken record—or maybe an endlessly repeated track on a CD! No matter what the symptomatic contention looks like in you, me, or us, the core value underlying any spiritual issue is *always* the same: Will we exchange a world that revolves around us for a world that revolves around God?

DISCUSSION QUESTIONS

Personal Discipleship

1. Where in your world do you feel the most contention from an *external* source?

2. Where in your world do you feel the most contention from an *internal* source?

3. At times, all Christians find themselves being a donkey caught in a wrestling match with God! In your experience, what has helped you to break out of these seasons of stubbornness?

4. What advice would you give a brand new Christian in regards to guarding against the attacks of the evil one?

5. Read Romans 7:15–20 and Paul's description of his own inner struggle. In what aspect of your life do you experience this same struggle?

Congregational Discipleship

1. Is there a pattern to the contention that has historically been present within your congregation? If so, what is it?

2. How do these issues compare and contrast to those that the Early Church experienced as described in the New Testament? Explain your answer.

3. Is there one or more issue(s) that is currently a flash point for debate within your church?

4. If your answer to 3 is yes, what are the underlying values that are at odds?

5. To what degree is your church united in its purpose to "invite... grow...send"? Is the term "bicultural" as defined in this chapter an accurate descriptor? Explain your response.

7

A Cooperative Process

We Are Not Alone

"If you love me, you will obey what I command. And I will ask the Father, and he will give you another Counselor."

JESUS (Jn. 14:15–16)

The concept of discipleship and being a disciple applies to both me individually and us collectively, and means responding to Jesus' invitation: "If anyone would come after me, he must deny himself and take up his cross daily and follow me" (Lk. 9:23). Discipleship is nothing less than a transformational, two-step process: *First,* we must let go of our world ("deny yourself"); *second,* we must embrace the kingdom of God ("follow me"). Again, true discipleship entails a radical shift of values: exchanging a world in which we are at the center for a world in which God is at the center; dying to sin and living for righteousness; putting off the things of the world and putting on the things of God. You have also come to see that discipleship is a lifelong process, a journey of faith with specific ongoing, relative, purposeful, and contentious dimensions. But if all I knew about discipleship were these four dimensions, I would be very discouraged. Though each is important and helpful to understand, when put together, they do not tell the whole story.

At this point, I need to pose a question: how is Christian discipleship unique and distinctive from discipleship found in other world religions? So far, many similarities seem to exist. All religions of the world have some standard of spirituality that followers are challenged to attain. Hinduism grapples with the nature of self. Buddhism struggles with the nature and cause of suffering. Islam seeks ways to submit to Allah, the creator. Animistic religions battle evil spirits. Christian discipleship resembles some aspect of each of these religions in that followers are called to maintain a certain attitude and accompanying lifestyle. Now, however, we take a different turn as I pose several more questions: What religion teaches that the Creator of the universe willingly endured human suffering and death to live within and empower faithful disciples? What religion teaches that God desires to serve us rather than expecting us to earn eternal blessings on our own? Only Christianity—no other religion— claims that God not only defines the desired lifestyle and standards, but provides the means to reach them.[1] Christian discipleship is not about jumping through hoops to earn a reward, but about trusting a God who indwells and enables people of faith to overcome their human shortcomings.

Personal Discipleship
God's Power from Within

This stunning truth of God's service to you and me brings us to one final, compelling dimension. Being a Christian disciple—exchanging my world for God's—is a *cooperative* partnership with the Creator, a reality that is clearly distinguishable from any other religion or worldview. Amazingly, our partner is the Spirit of the living God, the power that can overcome all human frailties or inadequacies. Unlike the followers of other religions, we are not striving to achieve a moral and/or ethical standard on our own. Rather, God has provided the means to realize our citizenship in the kingdom—*if* we love Christ. The Holy Spirit is that vital means.

For many, the person of the Holy Spirit is the most difficult aspect of God to envision and understand. Parental images help many of us to grasp God's character and role. Of course, the person and nature of Jesus is the easiest to grab hold of since He walked among us: the Word made flesh is quite tangible! In sharp contrast, the Spirit is an invisible force much like the wind. We can fathom the Spirit's influence, but we cannot see or measure this godly power, for who can control the wind? We are further challenged in that the Bible contains relatively few verses that describe the Holy Spirit.

The clearest and most comprehensive passage on the Spirit's character and role is found in the Gospel of John, during Jesus' upper room discourse directed to His disciples (Jn. 13–16). In the final days of His earthly ministry, Jesus emphasizes the Spirit—the One who would guide them in the future. Jesus unashamedly states that His leaving is a benefit for his band of followers: "I tell you the truth, anyone who has faith in me will do what I have been doing. He will do even greater things than these, because I am going to the Father" (14:12). Jesus clearly tells his disciples that after His departure, the Spirit "will be in you" (14:17). The Spirit has been with them before, but that same Spirit will soon be very active in their lives, empowering them to do those "great things" that Jesus alludes to. From the day of the Spirit's arrival on Pentecost, the apostles see this promise realized in spades: They experience this awesome inner power spurring them onward (Acts 1,2).

Continuing to shed light on this cooperative Partner, Jesus spells out additional truths about the Spirit. In a nutshell, "holy" describes both the Spirit's character and function. This Spirit is holy and makes us holy. Whereas Jesus has died for us, the Spirit lives in us. Jesus' work on the cross puts us right with God; the Spirit's work in our hearts seeks to make us holy like God. We are forgiven through Christ's work; we are transformed through the Spirit's. God's Spirit—our Partner—enables us to overcome our addiction to self-interest—to wanting to live in a world in which we are at the center. How do we cooperate with the Spirit? How can we daily benefit from our Partner's strength and power as we struggle to let go of this world and follow Jesus? Our Master tells us the secret; He lays out the very key to unlocking the Spirit's work in and through us: "If you love me, you will obey what I command. And I will ask the Father, and he will give you another Counselor" (Jn. 14:15–16). The condition for the Spirit's coming is love for the King, the kind of love that evokes obedience, the kind of love that willingly cooperates.

An Image of Cooperation

At an early age, I learned a simple truth about wind: it moves from high pressure to low pressure—from the point of most resistance to the point of least resistance. A middle school science teacher brought this truth alive for me one day with a basic round balloon. He inflated the balloon to its capacity so that the air on the inside was under greater pressure than the air on the outside. He then released the balloon without tying off the opening. I bet you can guess what happened next. The air streaming out of the opening propelled the balloon around the room—noisily! This experiment helped me to see that the air quickly moved from the inside (high pressure) to the outside (low pressure). With the insights of the Old and New Testament, we learn that the Spirit—whose root words in both Hebrew and Greek mean "wind"—also moves from high to low pressure. God's power moves from the point of most resistance to the point of least resistance. When our souls tend toward "high pressure," we become resistant to the work of God in our lives. Predictably, the Holy Spirit respects our right to be stubborn and allows us to wallow in our sinful and self-centric ways. Like a sailboat that eventually becomes marooned without a breeze, our journey of faith slows to a dead crawl.

On the other hand, when "low pressure" marks our spiritual lives, we demonstrate the opposite: an eagerness to cooperate with what God's Spirit is seeking to do in our lives. Low-pressure disciples feel the wind—God's power—at their back, propelling them gently, or not so gently, as they take their next steps of faith. Low-pressure disciples realize that they cannot let go of the world's values and embrace God's kingdom apart from the Holy Spirit's power. They know that real transformation occurs only when they harness the enormous "wind" power of the Holy Spirit. Simply stated, low-pressure disciples let God be God—*they cooperate as they repent, believe, and obey!* So the choice for disciples is obvious: do we cooperate with God and allow the Holy One's power to spur our ongoing exchange of worlds, or do we try to live life on our own? Do we seek to be low-pressure followers who are open to God's Spirit, or do we become high-pressure "Lone Rangers" who depend upon ourselves? These inquiries naturally lead us to other practical concerns: If we do want to see the Holy Spirit work powerfully in our lives, which deliberate steps and strategies do we map out so we can initiate and maintain "low pressure" in our hearts and minds?

Let's see how the process of becoming kingdom citizens is cooperative for the individual disciple. We will also explore the practical strategies that foster cooperative, low-pressure hearts.

Spiritual Disciplines: The Proven Avenue for Fostering Low Pressure

For centuries, godly men and women have engaged in specific practices that stir our hearts to repent and believe—the pathway to low-pressure hearts. These have come to be known as *spiritual habits* or *spiritual disciplines.* Though Jesus and numerous biblical figures have modeled these disciplines, many Christians remain fuzzy with respect to the important role of spiritual disciplines.[2] I subdivide the various disciplines into three categories based on their purpose—strengthening my relationship with God, guiding my relationship with other believers, and realizing my responsibility to God's world. This division helps me grasp and remember the benefit of practicing the disciplines. Here's how I describe them:

- *My relationship with God* is strengthened as I exercise the disciplines of *prayer* and the *study of God's Word.* These habits encourage me to keep God and the kingdom as the cornerstone of my life.
- *My relationship with other Christians* is guided and enhanced as I exercise the disciplines of *worship* and *fellowship.* These habits weave me into the Christian community—a vital means to sustain my own faithfulness and encourage the faithfulness of others.
- *My responsibility to God's world* is realized through the disciplines of *service* and *generosity.* As I share my God-given talents as well as my financial resources, the Spirit uses them to make a difference in my heart as well as in the world.

Before proceeding, let's look more closely at how the disciplines work. Let's consider prayer. Does God desire that we pray to keep Him posted with what is going on in our lives? Of course not! Our sovereign God knew us even before we were knitted in our mothers' wombs (Ps. 139:13). The value of prayer is that it transforms *me*. When I pray, I am acknowledging that God is God and I am not. That's a crucifixion–of me, my will, and my self-importance. If I am not careful, the discipline of prayer will result in a change of attitude. That all-important heart attitude helps to make me a low-pressure, pliable, and obedient disciple. (Some of the Psalms are great examples of this principle. They begin with grumbling and end with praise. Try Psalm 13 or 22 for this perspective.) Consider the discipline of generosity. Did God establish the practice of tithing to create cash flow for Christ's Church? No, God designed it to create wind flow–the Spirit's wind–through our hearts. The discipline of giving is not about the need of any church to receive my money, but about my need to release the clutch I have on my "stuff."

Spiritual Disciplines: Prescriptions from the Master Doctor

When I am sick and make the deliberate trip to see a doctor, I am making an implicit statement: I realize that I am not healthy and I need professional help. Typically, the doctor will go through some diagnostic process even if he or she has a strong inkling about my condition. I have come to anticipate that the good doc will check my pulse, poke around in orifices, measure my blood pressure, and listen to the whirring and clicking of various internal organs. Eventually, the doctor pulls all the related data together and draws a conclusion about what I need to do. The result is always some kind of action plan–a prescription. It's a practical strategy, but not an end unto itself. It is simply a means by which the natural healing powers of the body can be promoted. All I have to do– and that's a big *all*–is to be faithfully obedient. I have to do two things: *trust* that the doctor really does know best, and *take* my prescription regularly.

As you can see, engaging in spiritual disciplines is a lot like filling and taking a doctor's prescription. Disciplines, however, are not divine currency that help me earn some heavenly blessing or achieve a certain behavioral standard. Rather, they are a *prescription* to be taken by faith. They serve to open my heart to the sanctifying winds of the Spirit. They foster, promote, and sustain a faithful and repentant heart so that the healing powers of the Spirit can be released. That's a key point. Taking the prescription (spiritual disciplines) faithfully helps my heart to be more pliable and willing to cooperate with the Spirit's work in my life. Cooperative transformation–exchanging worlds–only occurs when repentance and faith are combined with the movement of God's powerful Spirit within me. Only *then* can the winds of the Spirit be at my back, pushing me gently but insistently as I take my next step of faith.

Emerging Truth about My Discipleship

In this ongoing process of exchanging my world for God's, I have a Holy Partner. To help me cultivate a low-pressure heart so that I can cooperate with this Partner, the Master Doctor has provided me with a prescription for godliness. Make no mistake about it, however: the primary objective of spiritual habits, practices, or whatever you want to call them is to break our love of self and deepen our love for God—a two-step process. With precision, the spiritual disciplines slowly chip away at my self-reliance and increasingly help me let God be God.

Let's review some key points about discipleship and add these bedrock principles to our understanding:

- *Discipleship is a cooperative process.* I am not alone as I faithfully follow the path of Christ.
- *The Spirit's role is to guide, mentor, counsel, empower, and renew.* Transformation is not a function of my own efforts, but is accomplished through the Spirit's power, which enables me to overcome the effects of sin in my life.
- *My role is to love Christ and faithfully obey.* If my heart is marked by low pressure, I give the Spirit permission and access to mold my character, attitudes, and actions.
- *Spiritual disciplines are the practical strategies to sustaining low pressure—a repentant and believing heart.* Like a good patient, I must take my prescription of study, prayer, fellowship, worship, service, and generosity. These disciplines are the proven, effective way to train for the marathon of faithful living.

Congregational Discipleship

A quick scan of the shelves at my local Christian bookstore tells me that the Holy Spirit's role in the believer's life is a hot topic. While I am grateful for this emphasis and hope that more Christians will understand and welcome the cooperative work of the Spirit, I have to wonder: What about churches? As described in the Introduction, I have been seeking answers to a handful of basic questions such as:

How can today's churches capture the same transforming power of the Holy Spirit that was clearly evident in the earliest Christian congregations? In other words, what fuels the movement of the Holy Spirit among God's gathered people? Why are some churches on fire while others are stone cold? And what–if anything–can faithful leaders do to turn their dying or stagnant churches around?

As we have seen, the cooperative dimension of discipleship provides us with many insights into understanding the movement of the Spirit in and through the individual followers of Christ. The local church must also understand its need of God's power and presence to fulfill its mission because true congregational discipleship can only occur through the cooperative partnership between the Spirit and the Body of Christ.

Movements of the Spirit

A survey of the history of God's work in the world beginning with Abraham reveals a constant state of spiritual flux for the people of faith. The pattern is painfully predictable: high pressure (dependence on self) followed by low pressure (dependence on God) followed again by high pressure, and so on. This ongoing cycle of renewal and decline seems to never end: we suffer the consequences of our sin; God intervenes; we recognize our need; we pray for renewal; God restores us; we lose sight of God's grace and our need; and we fall back into old habits. For our purposes, let's quickly review a few examples from Scripture that will help us understand what promotes and fosters low pressure among God's people.

An Old Testament Movement

God commissioned Joshua to lead Israel into the promised land after Moses' death. He and thousands of people found themselves on the banks of the swollen Jordan River (Josh. 2–3). Crossing the Jordan–at flood stage–was the necessary first step for Israel to begin claiming the land of Canaan, collectively. Joshua knew well the power of the Spirit of God, for he gave an order to the people: "Consecrate yourselves, for tomorrow the Lord will do amazing things among you" (Josh. 3:5). Two things stand out in Joshua's words. First, he instructs the people to get ready for a great and holy presence among them. Second, he acknowledges that it is God–not Joshua himself, not a civil engineer who could throw up a makeshift bridge, not even the priests from the Levite tribe–who would empower the Israelites to accomplish the task ahead of them. You know the rest of the story. The people broke camp with low-pressure hearts and followed the Ark of the Covenant of God, which the priests carried to the very edge of the water. As the priests stepped in, the water piled up upon itself. Dare I suggest that a holy wind blew on the muddy bottom of the Jordan, drying up the muck and enabling the people of God to take their next steps of faith as they crossed the river?

On this occasion, Israel collectively recognized her need and relied upon God's holy power. The people of God quite literally walked by faith and put their complete hope in God rather than in themselves. The winds of the Holy Spirit were evident and strong. In time, however, the cyclical pattern of their loyalty returned, and the power of God was quenched as they relied on their own cunning and wisdom. (See the Book of Judges.) Their hearts became high-pressure havens. The Spirit's winds could no longer propel them, "everyone did as he saw fit" (Judg. 21:25).

NEW TESTAMENT WINDS

The epitome of spiritual low pressure is the day of Pentecost. Jesus' final instructions before His ascension leave no doubt that the wind of holy power will soon indwell His followers: "Do not leave Jerusalem, but wait for the gift my Father promised, which you have heard me speak about. For John baptized with water, but in a few days you will be baptized with the Holy Spirit" (Acts 1:4a-5). By this time, the apostles are ready and willing to be obedient to their Lord, Christ the King. In keeping with their love and reliance upon Him, they comply and prayerfully wait. When the time is right–fifty days after the resurrection–the Holy Spirit not only arrives but takes up residence in their hearts. Immediately, this very Spirit of God fulfills the words of Jesus to "take from what is mine and make it known to you" (Jn. 16:15b). The apostles preach the Good News in languages they have never learned. Thousands of amazed listeners gathered in Jerusalem respond by faith. Many are healed emotionally, spiritually, and physically. A sense of unity and community exists among the new believers across all sociological boundaries. Believers and nonbelievers alike could see the winds of change. At the center of their world is not a thing, but a loyal allegiance to a Person who sits on a throne.

SPIRITUAL AWAKENINGS SINCE PENTECOST

Richard Lovelace comprehensively explores the nature of spiritual awakenings throughout church history. Not surprisingly, he discovers the Holy Spirit is not bound by time, geography, or theological perspective. When the hearts and minds of God's people are compliant and cooperative, the Spirit moves with power in and through faithful servants. Lovelace isolates preconditions that have been consistently present before the onset of a revival. His work describes two in detail: (1) a widespread awareness of the depth of sin (both individually and corporately), and (2) an awareness of the holiness of God (His justice and love). In other words, times of spiritual renewal have historically been preceded by an overwhelming recognition that God is God and we are not.[3]

Step One of Congregational Transformation

These biblical and historical precedents reinforce that this whole concept of congregational vitality is actually pretty simple and can be boiled down to one central issue: Is Jesus Christ Lord? When Jesus is increasingly the Head of a church with respect to its message and methods, and when its people seek to be godly servants to these priorities, the Spirit's wind is strong, the power of sinful addictions is broken over time, and God's grace is evident to all. True discipleship will always lead a church to bend its collective knee to Jesus and infuse the body of Christ with the promised Holy Spirit. On the other hand, when a congregation invests energy in serving itself and views Jesus as merely a respected peer or advisor, the influence of selfish interests gradually erodes kingdom values, and the Spirit's power diminishes.

Again, Jesus could not have spelled out His will and desire for His people any more clearly: "If you love me, you will obey what I command. And I will ask the Father, and He will give you another Counselor" (Jn. 14:15–16). The precondition for spiritual renewal, transformation, and systemic change is exchanging our world for Christ's—loving His priorities and ways more than ours. As we have seen, this process of moving toward Christ as the center of our collective lives is ongoing, relative, purposeful, contentious, and, thankfully, cooperative.

As noted in the Introduction, I am not suggesting that those interested in the renewal and transformation of the local church should avoid the study of behavioral science. I would even say that encouraging any change in a church's culture apart from a working knowledge of change management principles would be foolish. For too long, pastors have failed to take advantage of social scientists' expertise as the necessary *second step* for understanding congregational dynamics. But I would also suggest that church leaders must acknowledge an absolutely vital *first step:* the starting point for any spiritual renewal and transformation depends upon the Holy Spirit's access to the congregation's heart. Our hearts are the thrones where Christ wants to live and reign as King. Therefore, the loyalty of our hearts is square one of transformation—the very foundation for enduring change and spiritual vitality. It is really quite simple: Congregations must repent, believe, and obey—changing the world God's way.

Keeping the Wind Blowing

As already noted, spiritual disciplines or practices are widely understood to be effective faith-building activities for individual disciples, the doctor's prescription for sustaining healthy hearts rightly aligned to the King's reign. In the same way, churches should be deliberate in taking practical steps to promote and sustain low-pressure–Christ-centeredness. In stating that spiritual disciplines exist for the local church, I am suggesting that congregations that desire collective spiritual vitality can engage in specific activities that will encourage cooperation with the transformational power of the Holy Spirit.[4] The combination of a church's obedience and the work of the Spirit is the essence of congregational discipleship–moving from a world in which we are the center to a world in which Christ is at the center. Drawing once again on Richard Foster's farming illustration (see Introduction), I believe that this cooperative effort combines our "sowing, weeding, and watering" with the grace and power of the Holy Spirit to effect a real change in our hearts. Let's take a moment to review a sampling of biblical and historical evidence supporting this concept.

WHAT GOD REALLY MEANT

I have always wanted to see some of the Old Testament stories real time–especially some excerpts from Abraham's life. I would love to see God confirm the covenant promise He previously made to Abraham that he would be the father of many nations (Gen. 12:1–3). I would also enjoy seeing Abraham throwing back his head and laughing as God tells him that, at 99 years of age, he will be a father through his barren wife Sarai. What I really want to check out is God telling Abraham about a brand new prescription for the father-to-be and his family: male circumcision. As Abraham's next step of faith, he, his son Ishmael (through Sarai's maidservant Hagar), and all the men of Israel are to be circumcised as a sign of the covenant–the agreement between God and Israel. (I want to hear Abraham's explain this one to the men and watch their reaction!) I believe that this rite was a forerunner of what we call spiritual disciplines today and was intended to function in a similar way to foster the work of God and encourage faithful obedience.

Circumcision was the first element of a more complete prescription for faithful living called the "Mosaic Law." In this, God expands on the circumcision ritual to provide His people with a comprehensive list of practical and spiritual disciplines (see Deuteronomy and Leviticus). The laws entrusted to Moses were designed to be a doctor's prescription–a set of guidelines for God's people to obey by faith, trusting that the Doctor knows best. Unfortunately, they were frequently turned into a job description–a series of man-imposed steps to earn God's blessing. (We see this distortion of God's intent in Jesus' contention with the Pharisees.) The people of Israel were supposed to follow God's laws faithfully and humbly, trusting in His guidance each step of the way. Instead, they frequently relied upon themselves—viewing their observance of the Law as a means by which they could obligate God to bless them.

THE EARLY CHURCH'S DISCIPLINES

The reality of congregational spiritual disciplines seems self-evident as we study the disciples who formed the earliest community of Christ. The activities of the Jerusalem church, as described in Acts, communicate a clear message about priorities:

> They devoted themselves to the apostles' teaching and to the fellowship, to the breaking of bread and to prayer. Everyone was filled with awe, and many wonders and miraculous signs were done by the apostles. All the believers were together and had everything in common. Selling their possessions and goods, they gave to anyone as he had need. Every day they continued to meet together in the temple courts. They broke bread in their homes and ate together with glad and sincere hearts, praising God and enjoying the favor of all the people. And the Lord added to their number daily those who were being saved. (2:42–47)

Preaching, worship, sharing, teaching, evangelism, fellowship, and prayer were among the many spiritual habits the early members of the church practiced to cultivate and sustain its spiritual vibrancy. Note they practiced these activities together as a unified, cooperative community, not as separate individuals. Again, engaging in these activities was not a means for these disciples, individually or collectively, to earn God's blessing, but a way to foster cooperation with God's ongoing work in their lives. Remember, the winds of God's Spirit flow from high pressure to low, from the point of most resistance to the point of least resistance. Faithfully practicing these disciplines fostered a low-pressure heart among this community of believers so God's power could transform their lives together.

CHURCH HISTORY

Richard Lovelace has ascertained not only the preconditions to renewal, but also those elements that have consistently emerged in the life of the Church to sustain the Spirit's ongoing work. He consistenely discovered the following evidence of faithfulness at times of revival:

- Mission: Following Christ into the world and presenting the Gospel
- Prayer: Expressing dependence on the power of the Spirit
- Community: Being in union with others within the church
- Disenculturation: Choosing freedom from cultural values
- Theological Integration: Having the mind of Christ

These five elements sure look like spiritual disciplines uniquely suited to promote faithfulness within a whole community.

Congregational Spiritual Disciplines

Like the disciples of the Early Church and throughout its history, we, as members of Christ's Church today, also have a need to engage in practices that serve to keep our hearts collectively receptive to the Spirit of God. The disciplines detailed below and in part 3 of this book should not be construed as an exhaustive list. Any number of initiatives and ministries can foster a congregation's openness to God. Certain congregational disciplines stand out because they are particularly valuable in promoting collective faithfulness, just as prayer is a core discipline for our individual journeys. In the same way that Richard Foster and others have provided various models to organize the individual disciplines, let me offer a three-pronged model for congregational disciplines.

- *Cornerstone* disciplines help secure Christ as Head of the Church and include
    - ~ cornerstone discernment
    - ~ leadership alignment
    - ~ vision casting
- *Ministry* disciplines help establish Christ's disciple-making methods and include
    - ~ relevant worship
    - ~ spiritual formation
    - ~ lay mobilization
- *Support* disciplines help provide Christ's mission and people with essential resources and include
    - ~ empowering systems
    - ~ aligned facilities
    - ~ generous stewardship[5]

In part 3, I will delve into each of these groupings and offer practical suggestions for all disciplines.

Emerging Truth about Our Discipleship

Chapter 1 explored the invitation to exchange a world in which I am at the center for a world in which God is at the center. The means of exchange involves two actions: letting go (dying to self or repentance) and embracing (living for Christ or believing). Then, in the first part of this chapter, we looked at the role the spiritual disciplines play in helping our hearts to remain open and cooperative with the Spirit's powerful movement to transform us into low-pressure disciples seeking to do the will of our King.

The congregational disciplines introduced in this chapter and detailed in part 3 outline practical steps to help churches also undergo this transformational, two-step process of repentance and belief. Each discipline, in its own way, encourages the body of Christ to exchange worlds by either eroding (letting go of) the temptation to be self-centered (hire...watch...pay values) or encouraging (embracing) the pursuit of kingdom priorities (invite...grow...send values). As these disciplines move the church's collective heart toward low pressure, the Spirit's power to transform moves in and through its members to accomplish the ultimate purpose of the Church—to make disciples.

As we review what we have learned about congregational discipleship, these bedrock principles will strengthen our perspective and understanding:

- *Congregational discipleship is a cooperative process.* We are not alone as we faithfully follow the path of Christ.
- *The Spirit's role is to guide, mentor, counsel, empower, and renew.* Transformation is not strictly a function of our own efforts. It is accomplished through the Spirit's power, which enables us to overcome the effects of sin within our community.
- *Step one of real and lasting congregational transformation begins with our hearts.* No change management principles, ministry programs, or how-to books will ever fully address the root question that every church must answer: Is Jesus Christ the King of our church?
- *Congregational spiritual disciplines, like personal disciplines, are meant to foster a congregation that repents and believes—low-pressure conduits for the Spirit's powerful winds.* The spiritual habits encouraged in the cornerstone, ministry, and support disciplines are effective ways to encourage our collective death to self and ongoing living for Christ.

At the end of the day, the truth underlying congregational discipleship is as profound as it is simple. Each church must choose which taste it prefers: Burger King ("have it your way") or King of kings (bow to His way). Any other decision a church makes will hinge on this one choice.

DISCUSSION QUESTIONS

Personal Discipleship

1. Identify a time in your life when you strongly sensed the presence of the Holy Spirit. What prompted this special relationship?
2. What aspect of the Holy Spirit's ministry is easiest to understand? What is the most difficult?

3. Which of the spiritual disciplines is most effective at helping you be a "low-pressure system"—open to the work of God? Why is that?

4. John 14:15–16 identifies the precondition for the Spirit's active presence in my life as a love for Christ. What are other words or phrases that could replace "love" and retain the same meaning? What new insights emerge from this exercise?

5. What is one practical step that you could take this day to lower the pressure of your heart?

Congregational Discipleship

1. Identify a time and place when you strongly sensed the power of God within a large group setting. From your standpoint, what attitude or action prompted this reality?

2. Imagine yourself being present in Jerusalem on the day of Pentecost. As one of Christ's disciples, what would have been your reaction? How would you have responded if you had been an outsider?

3. Over the past year, when did you sense that the winds of the Spirit were strongest? To what do you attribute this?

4. From your perspective, describe what you sense Christ is calling your congregation to let go of and embrace at this time.

5. Before you read part 3, what congregational discipline seems strongest in your congregation? weakest?

PART III

Spiritual Disciplines for Us

Intentional Strategies That Promote Spiritual Vitality

Practicing congregational disciplines encourages Christ's churches to be engaged in a transformational process: letting go of their own agenda and embracing the redemptive work that God is seeking to accomplish in and through their communities—the essence of congregational faithfulness.

8

Cornerstone Disciplines

Securing Christ as Head of the Church

Consequently, you are no longer foreigners and aliens, but fellow citizens with God's people and members of God's household, built on the foundation of the apostles and prophets, with Christ Jesus himself as the chief cornerstone.

PAUL (Eph. 2:19–20)

Congregational faithfulness can be defined as the journey of a community of Christ followers gradually letting go of its self-serving ways and willingly embracing Jesus' next steps of faith. So, how hard can this two-step transformational process be for a group of imperfect people? Unfortunately, a collective process of dying to self and living for Christ is not only incredibly difficult, it is very rare. Hence the obvious question: What can a church's leadership possibly do or say to promote a constant realignment of priorities? In other words, what practical strategies will encourage a group of disciples to increasingly exchange their agenda for Jesus'?

As I have repeatedly suggested, a radical change of priorities or culture can only be realized through a cooperative process: we till, sow, and water while God simultaneously grows the church's heart. From my vantage point, congregational transformation must begin with a church body deliberately securing Christ as its Head, thus becoming the "cornerstone" for every church matter. Let me explain this cornerstone principle and its three related disciplines, the backbones that make ongoing transformation possible.

The First Cornerstone: Image

I first encountered the principle of a cornerstone when I noticed Paul's reference to one in his letter to the Ephesians. I learned that in ancient times a builder would begin the house construction process by precisely positioning the first stone, called the cornerstone. Once in place, this stone became the guide for vertical and horizontal plumb. If the walls, floor, and roof were all aligned to this one guiding stone, the entire house would be square. In calling Christ the "chief cornerstone" (2:20), Paul is suggesting that Jesus is the standard to which disciples should align their lives. He is the kingdom of God cornerstone that allows us to square our lives to the Creator's "Garden of Eden" culture. For individual disciples, the notion of aligning one's faith walk to kingdom principles–as exemplified by Jesus–is relatively straightforward and the essence of the popular WWJD (What Would Jesus Do) wristband.

Learning from One of the Best

With respect to communities, I learned a great deal about the cornerstone principle as general manager and president of a multisite retail business with sixty-five employees. At the time of my hiring, this family business had long ago lost alignment to its founder's cornerstone values. It was on the brink of bankruptcy. As an outsider, I knew my job was to restore its original culture and corresponding values and, in so doing, its profitability. Along the way, I unexpectedly witnessed one of the premier secular examples of cornerstone alignment. My cornerstone-in-action experience occurred when a vendor invited me to attend a presentation at the Ritz-Carlton in Detroit. Well, this boy from Texas had never even seen a Ritz-Carlton. I was pretty impressed. What really caught my attention was the way I was treated. Within several hours of arriving, I left my room to attend a program meeting held in a first floor conference room. As I passed through the lobby, one of the concierges called: "Good evening, Mr. Halley." I was shocked and surprised. Was I in trouble? How did this guy know my name?

Several hours later, I received another jolt as I passed through the lobby on my way back to my room. Another concierge said, "Good night, Mr. Halley." Thinking, "Okay, this is weird," I thanked him and kept on going. As I neared my room on the third floor, I encountered yet another Ritz-Carlton employee, with the now-predictable, "Sleep well, Mr. Halley." That did it! I stopped him in his tracks and asked him to explain what was going on. Politely, he coached me on the values, beliefs, vision, and mission of Ritz-Carlton hotels. He proudly said, "Our motto is: '*We are Ladies and Gentlemen Serving Ladies and Gentlemen.*'" He showed me a small pocket tri-fold that detailed the hotel chain's credo, mission, values, and service principles. Calling guests by their names is a top value at the Ritz. The front desk employees had discreetly taken my picture upon my arrival and passed it around. Color me impressed! Getting the leaders of a large string of hotels to define and publish the organization's values and mission is one thing. Incarnating those values on a day-to-day basis—particularly on the third floor of just one of the many Ritz-Carlton hotels—is a whole other issue. I still have that tri-fold and continue to share this little story quite often to make a point. What I learned that day and through numerous subsequent experiences is that all organizations—including the local church—benefit from a well-defined and owned cornerstone. Just like the Ritz-Carlton, living out one's articulated cornerstone is an ongoing, never-ending process of alignment.

Learning from the Master

As a church leader for twenty-five years, I have also come to see the importance of these cornerstone principles for Jesus' church. As much as I have learned about this concept from business experiences, textbooks, and life coaches, my real mentor on the subject of fostering a kingdom-based community is the Master Himself. I should have seen it much earlier, because Jesus was a genius at cornerstone craftsmanship. His example is spelled out in detail within the gospels. As He repeatedly teaches and models the four sides of a community's cornerstone, Jesus demonstrates:

- *Values* that define *what is important* and describe who God is calling us to be. (Many of His parables as well as His actions spell these out in detail.)
- *Beliefs* that define *what is essential* and describe the nonnegotiable truths of faith communities. (The Sermon on the Mount and other discourses define the essentials of our faith—the Early Church's "apostles' teaching" referenced in Acts 2:42.)
- *Vision* that defines *where we are going* and describes the God-inspired calling of the church. (In Acts 1:8, Jesus shares a vision of taking the gospel to the ends of the earth.)
- *Mission* (or purpose) that defines *how we will get there* and describes the process by which disciples will fulfill Christ's agenda. (Jesus gives a clear directive in the "Great Commission" of Mt. 28:18–20.)[1]

Even though Jesus does not organize these four aspects of the cornerstone on a handy laminated tri-fold, He does leave His followers instructions which are crystal clear. Not only was He exceptional at communicating these principles, He was extraordinarily effective at embedding them into His disciples. Here we are two thousand years later, and we are still studying His words and seeking to live them out. So why should a twenty-first–century congregation take the time and effort to intentionally define, affirm, and validate a kingdom-based cornerstone?

The Spiritual Benefits of Congregational Cornerstones

The principle is rather simple: congregational cornerstones—personalized definitions of a God-centered church—help to secure Christ as the church's Head. In so doing, a cornerstone answers critical questions such as *What is important? What is essential? Where are we going?* and *How will we get there?* This intentional, culture-creating focus is *not* strategic planning or a decision made and implemented; it is nothing less than a church's deepening agreement with the values of Christ—a gradual transformation of culture. As congregations stay grounded and focused on Christ, they can increasingly understand God's design for the Church and for their own specific fellowship of believers, taking on the blessed role of servants discerning the will of the King.

Why is having a cornerstone so helpful in sustaining spiritual vitality? Well, do you remember the continuum in chapter 1, with the kingdom of God on one end and the world and its self-serving agenda on the other? That imagery underscores our inherent love and promotion of ourselves. We are the ultimate value in our own world, and the world that we naturally and readily desire is self-centric. (For churches, that looks like the *hire…watch…pay* model discussed in chapter 5.) To be faithful disciples, therefore, we have to repent—literally turn away from ourselves and embrace kingdom values (again, for churches, the *invite…grow…send* values). So, a church's cornerstone serves as a WWJD bracelet, a constant reminder of Jesus' values and priorities. What bracelet should encircle a church's wrist? I like WWCCD— *What Would Christ's Church Do?* Unfortunately, we are very tempted to treat these four cornerstone elements as one-time goals to be accomplished, hung on the wall, and forgotten. If properly understood, though, they begin a never-ending learning (once again, the root meaning of the word *disciple*) process and serve to constantly remind both new and mature disciples of kingdom priorities. Church consultants Bill Easum and Tom Bandy describe these cornerstones as the "DNA" of the church—an apt description. The challenge is to constantly infuse this kingdom DNA into every nook and cranny within the church community so that it exudes the personality of the King.

With this foundation, let me detail the three cornerstone disciplines that church leaders can exercise, which will foster obedience to Jesus—the linchpin to spiritual vitality.

Three Cornerstone Disciplines
The Discipline of Cornerstone Discernment

The first of the cornerstone disciplines—*cornerstone discernment*—focuses on the process by which the church's identity or DNA is initially established and sustained over time. Regrettably, many congregations adopt secular models for crafting and managing these foundational definitions. Even though churches and for-profit organizations share common ground in the *benefits* of having cornerstones, I am convinced that the *approaches* of the two need to be very different. Let me detail the differences.

First, I recommend that churches focus on discerning (a spiritual exercise) rather than deciding (a worldly exercise). As Christians, we live in two worlds. In our kingdom of God world, we are servants. As such, we are to discern or learn the King's design for our lives—a monarchy. In our earthly, American world, we are deciders or voters who exercise our freedom to self-determine our own direction—a democracy. Unfortunately, many church planning models fail to reflect the reality that Jesus is a King and that we need to be discerning rather than deciding.

Second, the process of discerning a church cornerstone should normally be bottom up, rather than top down. Most for-profit planning processes begin with a very small leadership core group that makes, announces, and disseminates key decisions. In contrast, the process of discerning a church's cornerstone ideally begins with—at minimum—the leadership community within the congregation (15–20 percent of its members), if not the entire congregation. The rationale for this approach is that this discernment process is a spiritual formation exercise and helps servants at all levels of participation learn what it means to be Christ's church.

Third, discerning a church cornerstone should begin with a focus on values, not vision. Generally speaking, secular organizations allow what they decide to *do* (vision) drive who they ultimately will *be* (values). For example, the pharmaceutical industry predictably adopts values congruent with its health-focused visions, while technology firms embrace values that predictably emphasize their desire to innovate. In contrast, the church ideally begins with a process to define the kingdom values it is being called to live out. In other words, who God has called us to *be* forms the basis for what we are called to *do*. (In the absence of biblical values, church visions frequently default to member-focused strategies.)

THE BENEFITS OF A BROAD-BASED APPROACH

Interestingly, a church's process of discerning a cornerstone is often as important as the cornerstone itself. Here's why. *First,* a broad-based discerning process is slower, and messier, than a top-down approach because it involves so many more people and time-consuming gatherings. While the top-down method may be appropriate for certain settings, such as in a new or unstable church, it is often less effective in a more established church. *Second,* a broad-based strategy builds a wider ownership for the church's future and greatly enhances the church's openness to new and related initiatives once the DNA is in place. *Third,* and most importantly, a church that opens the process to its active participants is setting the stage for greater faithfulness to Christ's mission. The coming together of core disciples to discern God-given values, beliefs, vision, and mission is a strong catalyst to the collective renewal of a church. Such a process predictably encourages congregants to set aside their preconceived notions and habits–letting go of their world–and rediscover who they are as a church of Jesus Christ–embracing a God-centered world.

THE KEY PRINCIPLES OF CORNERSTONE DISCERNMENT

As a core leadership team meets together to design a cornerstone discernment strategy that promotes congregational discipleship, it needs to bear in mind these relevant principles:

- *Patiently Discern, Don't Quickly Decide:* Designing a process to discern a Christ-centered cornerstone is more difficult than you might expect. One difficulty lies in the fact that many lay leaders–and pastors for that matter–are steeped in business models that focus on deciding rather than discerning. As already noted, another difficulty lies in timing: a discerning model is not a matter of adding water and stirring. It is a time-consuming, spiritual formation process that needs and benefits from plenty of participation and communication. In almost any setting expect the discernment process to take at least nine months, if not longer. Be patient!

- *Honor the Church's Established Culture:* As much as possible, the process should honor the church's established culture. (Exceptions to this rule do exist, particularly in a congregation dominated by a handful of controllers.) The process should recognize and "play ball" within the boundaries of the church's institutional systems. Obviously, a failure to do so tends to de-legitimize the entire exercise.

- *Include the "People of Passion."* Church consultant George Bullard makes a helpful distinction between those who have formal power–*the people of position*–and those who are the informal, influential leaders–*the people of passion.*[2] Predictably, an effective process must honor not only those with formal power, but also the primary participants who support the ministry both with their time and financial resources–the people of passion. Who are these folks in your setting? Get a church roster, gather a handful of active leaders together, and turn them loose. Ask them to identify the opinion makers who make the church happen. In short order, they will have identified 15+ percent of the church who likely support most of the budget. In fact, confidential giving records are one of the quickest ways to get a running start in building this list. The bottom line is this: the process needs to honor both the people of passion and the people of position.

- *Honor the Pastor:* Ideally, each stage of discernment will include the church's pastor(s) as a central part of the process. In so doing, the final cornerstone affirmations and related vision will have the unequivocal support of the pastor(s), who is a key spokesperson(s) and representative(s) of the church's cornerstone. Interestingly, this process may illuminate the existence of an ideological gap between the pastor and the church's membership. If differences present themselves, the process may need to be slowed down to find consensus before proceeding. Acknowledging and bridging an existing gap are goals in and of themselves. If the church's staff and membership do not share a common alignment to Christ's kingdom principles, how can the church even begin to expect the Spirit's winds at its back? If a shared, Christ-centered cornerstone is not in place, the discernment of one is the starting point for encouraging Christ-centeredness.

- *Customize Whatever Model You Adopt:* Multiple strategies for discerning a God-centered cornerstone exist. By the time this book is published, there will be even more. At present, I believe Tom Bandy's model detailed in his book *Moving Off the Map* is one of the most comprehensive of these strategies and can easily be tweaked to fit most churches. As you review his approach or any others, however, be ready to make adjustments that will fit your context.

- *Link the Planning Team with an Experienced Mentor:* A planning team will need to be empowered to guide the process. It will greatly benefit if it has an experienced coach. (This person could be a professional consultant or an experienced leader from a seasoned church.) As one who has been both a full- and part-time church consultant, I am well aware of the challenges of convincing a church board to invest in an outside coach for a task such as discerning a cornerstone. If this is the case in your setting, you may want to review how much money was spent on an architect for the last building project. The investment cost of a "cornerstone coach" is substantially less than an architect for a tangible cornerstone. Ultimately the benefit of a clear and owned "cornerstone" far outweighs the value of an attractive building.

- *Keep the Planning Team Focused on Process:* A business-oriented "deciding" model tends to pull together a representative collection of high rollers who "guide" the outcome. In most cases, this group consists of primary decision-makers who exert substantial influence. With a kingdom-oriented discernment approach, the planning team needs to be more focused on guiding the process than controlling the outcome. With a discernment process, the Head of the Church, namely Christ, already guides much of the outcome—especially the values and beliefs already detailed in the Scriptures. Accordingly, the planning team should focus its primary attention on building consensus and ownership.

- *Sustain Congregational Communication:* The secular marketing phrase "multiple mediums, maximum redundancy" is wise counsel for a church engaged in a discernment exercise. Though it may seem like overkill to insiders, a steady stream of updates and information is vital to keep the process open. Without it, the process can easily look like a prototypical business model with its smoked-filled rooms.

- *Create Multiple Cornerstone Images:* Multiple, tangible expressions of the cornerstone are critical to complete the discernment process. They include written core values, logos, mission statements, mottoes, vision statements, slogans, theme songs, statements of faith, and related symbols. (In each case, you want these summary statements and symbols to be memorable and transferable. If the sixth graders can recite and explain them, you are on target!) Like the cornerstone of ancient buildings, these declarations, sounds, and images remind a church of its basic reasons for *being* a church and become the common reference points to encourage a congregation's balance and alignment. They define both the vertical (worshiping God) and horizontal (serving others) plumb for the ministries of the church and provide continuous guidance to church leaders.

- *Expect Shifts in the Vision:* Once a generation of church disciples discerns and articulates its kingdom-centered values, beliefs, and mission, it will most likely not make significant changes to the definitions any time soon. All three of these elements are biblically grounded and predictably look alike from one Christian church to another. (The most critical shifts will come internally as the congregational leaders realign themselves to the cornerstone as opposed to their own agenda.) The church's vision, however, is another matter. By design, it is more time sensitive since it typically has a specified duration. Naturally, it will need to be revisited over and over again. Like our own life journey with new and emerging directions, a church must periodically stop and design a process to listen for the heartbeat of God.

PRAYER—A CRITICAL INGREDIENT

I would be remiss if I did not highlight prayer and its critical role in the discernment process. Predictably, a process that emphasizes listening to the King of kings will naturally make prayer a top priority. The Early Church was a praying church—an immensely important activity when you consider how easily the first movement of Christ's Church could have come to a screeching halt. Prayer is one of the central avenues by which God molds and shapes His people. If we are not praying for discernment, we have all but decided that we don't need or want God's direction and power. Unfortunately, many of us are prone to pounce on action items rather than spend time reflecting and discerning the will of the King.

I have learned much about the power of prayer from James Wessels, a godly pastor from the Midwest who, over the course of his years in ministry, has seen too many churches create their own plans and then ask God to bless them. Within his own ministry, Jim has learned the importance of making prayer a starting point for any planning process. The benefits of Jim's perspective and approach are simple to comprehend: God blesses whatever He asks His people to accomplish. To that end, Jim calls for "seasons of prayer" among his church members, some of which last a week, and some of which extend over several months. Journaling is an important part of this prayer process. At Jim's church, a room dedicated to prayer contains a journal during these special times. The notebook provides a common place for the people in prayer to record their leadings and insights. When members have these promptings—whether at home, church, or wherever—they are encouraged to write them down in the journal at the church. At the end of the prayer season, the church elders read the journal together to see what themes repeatedly emerge. The several stories Jim shared with me involving such intentional prayer were truly inspirational. In a democracy, voters decide, with the majority ruling. In the kingdom, with Christ as King, we are called to be servants and discern the Master's will. Prayer and quiet reflection are vital habits that help the church stay in touch with the King.

A QUICK SUMMARY

From the outset, I have been portraying discipleship as an exchange of worlds: trading in our current residence for a better one. Letting go of one set of values for another. Turning our backs on a culture that is self-centered for a new culture that is Christ-centered. The cornerstone is, in fact, a congregation's understanding of that new destination. It is the church's tailor-made WWJD bracelet. Accordingly, when properly exercised, the discipline of *cornerstone discernment* is a powerful means to encourage a church's core disciples to exchange a member-centered definition of congregational life for a Christ-centered paradigm that is grounded in the Great Commission. When the church's leadership defines its cornerstone—as expressed through values, beliefs, vision, and mission—the stage is then set for affirming Jesus as King, fostering humble servants, and releasing the power of God's Spirit.

The Discipline of Leadership Alignment

Once a kingdom-centered cornerstone is in place, the second cornerstone discipline must be permanently prioritized, namely leadership alignment. This discipline is the habit of building a core community of disciple-makers who recognize Jesus' rightful place on the throne of their church and are eager to embrace the discerned priorities. Again, Jesus, in His infinite wisdom, understood exactly how to accomplish this task. He could have tried to build a strong leadership core through utilizing large crusades, but He didn't. He could have chosen to build a mega-organization with the apostles as the leaders, but He didn't. He could have written manuals for His core disciples, but He didn't. Instead, He formed a community of passionate followers, embedded the kingdom DNA in their souls and spirits, paved the way for the indwelling power of God, and then got out of their way. The result: a community of core disciples who embraced His cornerstone and replicated His model of disciple-making ministry to the "ends of the earth."

BIRTHING A LEADERSHIP COMMUNITY

Those who desire to walk in Jesus' path and initiate such a leadership community should keep several foundational principles in mind.

Begin by clearly defining the attributes and actions of disciple-making leaders within your context. Disciples need and benefit from a clear understanding of what seasoned followers look like—both practically and conceptually. Obviously, Paul's letters to Timothy are a resounding affirmation of this truth and are a good place for any church to begin (see 1 Tim. 3). When adequately defined, these standards become a helpful means for leaders—along with respected mentors—to spiritually assess community members' progress and more clearly discern their next developmental steps as they live into their full kingdom potential.

Second, carefully select the right language as you form this core community. In my current setting, Paul's term "ambassador" (2 Cor. 5:18ff) has been introduced as a replacement for the term *leader*. An ambassador is defined as a disciple-making disciple and embodies the spiritual growth process (see appendix 1). The reason for this shift is simple: when staff members use the term "leader," many laity easily misunderstand our intent. By using "ambassador," we are encouraging all those who desire to be disciple-making disciples–regardless of their spiritual gifts and natural abilities–to become a part of our core community. Before this linguistic shift, we found that many strong disciples would avoid "leadership" training opportunities and events because they did not perceive themselves as having the "gift of leadership." We now emphasize ambassadorship and a related "learning community."

Third, embrace intentionality as a key ingredient. The existence of a strong and vibrant community of ambassadors is far from an accident. The formation of this community demands an enormous amount of focused human energy, is the most important priority of the church staff, only exists through the power of God's Spirit, and is the single biggest threat to the evil one. If your own personal experience does not corroborate this principle, you need only explore the priorities of Jesus' life and the way He used His time to fully appreciate this reality.

THE KEY PRINCIPLES OF LEADERSHIP ALIGNMENT

As a core leadership team meets together to design a leadership alignment strategy that promotes congregational discipleship, it needs to bear in mind these relevant principles:

- *Begin with Staff Modeling:* Lay leaders will not embrace what they do not see. If the staff team does not live out the principles and spirit of the church's kingdom-centered cornerstone, the successful formation of a leadership community is highly unlikely. George Cladis's *The Team-Based Church* is an insightful text on this subject and details how a church staff can discern and benefit from its own cornerstone that compliments the church's.[3] Staff cornerstone development is a strategy that, as an executive director and church consultant, I highly recommend as a means to encourage a kingdom-aligned staff (see appendix 2).
- *Establish Discernment as the Means for Discovering Group Consensus:* Leadership communities dedicated to serving the King are most effective when they discern, rather than decide, their next steps of faith. (Spiritual discernment is nothing more than knowing and doing God's will.) To implement this process among all leadership teams, three preconditions need to exist among the participants: (1) a relationship with God that includes candid dialogue, (2) a desire to know the will of God, and (3) a commitment to do the will of God. Once in place, leadership groups can discover consensus if all the

members, when discussing a specific issue, can arrive at one of three statements: (1) "I agree," (2) "I don't agree with everything, but I can live with it," or (3) "I don't agree at all, but I can see that most do agree and I can live with it." If one member of the group cannot make one of these three statements, the process of prayerful discernment continues.[4]

- *Schedule Regular Gatherings of Ambassadors:* Getting the core disciples together on a regular basis is key to cultivating a leadership community. Normally, these events will have the feel of worship and creatively combine elements such as singing, dramas, slide shows, special speakers, inspiration, recognition of ministry achievement, testimonies, laughing, commissioning, surprises, vision casting, and targeted training—all linked to the church's cornerstone. Within my current congregation, these gatherings are called "*Four:Twelve*" based on Ephesians 4:12, and occur 4–5 times a year. These gatherings are mandatory for the people of position as well as the ambassadors of all ministry areas and are open to aspiring ambassadors throughout the church community.[5]

- *Make Outsiders Insiders by Providing Consistent Communication:* Throughout the year and as needed, staff leaders should distribute a supplemental communiqué targeted to ambassadors to keep the community informed of emerging trends, upcoming initiatives, scheduling details, and related updates. The frequency of distribution is driven by the number of leadership gatherings—the fewer number of large-group gatherings, the greater the need for these periodic updates. Within my congregation, we typically distribute these "ministry briefings" monthly.

- *Plan Special Events to Energize the Community:* Over time, leadership communities need specially called gatherings that focus on pertinent matters. Annual retreats for ambassadors are a new tradition in my setting, but we also gather as needed to wrestle with issues such as land purchases, building expansion, and new missional initiatives. Together, we seek to hear a fresh message of hope and discern the church's next steps of faith.

- *Provide Ambassadors with Multiple Training Opportunities:* The development of a leadership community includes learning opportunities and strategies designed to enable disciples to achieve their own kingdom potential–"ambassadorship." Biblical education, targeted skill training, and especially experience with a mentor/coach are all effective strategies for achieving this goal. Ideally, this highly intentional process is also competency-based and builds on those things that ambassadors-in-training already understand. (This topic will be discussed further in the next chapter.)

- *Align Organizational Systems:* As one would expect, for the leadership community to be effective and efficient, the organizational systems of the church need to be aligned to the cornerstone. Form follows function. This truth is beautifully modeled by the example of the Early Church (Acts 15). The success of Paul and Barnabas in winning the lost Gentiles (form) ultimately shaped the perceptions and principles of the Jerusalem leaders (function). Chapter 10 will explore this concept in much more depth.

- *Promote Small Group Learning:* Though all the above strategies are helpful and useful, the DNA of the church—its values, beliefs, mission, and vision—is best caught in a dynamic, well-led, small-group setting. As a result, core staff leaders are well advised to initiate and constantly sustain a learning process within their teams that enables participants to fully understand the church's defined identity. With time, the number of leaders embedded with DNA will reach critical mass and usher in a whole new level of congregational faithfulness. The next section provides a great example of this strategy in more detail.

EMBEDDING THROUGH A SMALL-GROUP STRATEGY

Many pathways exist for transmitting a kingdom virus, but let me tell you about one in particular. Leith Anderson, a well-respected pastor who has written several helpful books about church life and the twenty-first century, spoke at a conference I attended several years back. He detailed a strategy that, from his perspective, was the most effective means for embedding a church's DNA that he had ever utilized—one that I am currently striving to emulate. In seeking to align his congregation to its stated values and mission, he invited 6–8 leaders at a time to learn, discuss, and explore with him what being a kingdom-focused church means. In advance, the participants would read several relevant books. They then met together for six consecutive weeks. Concurrently, each would also visit and complete an assessment of another nearby church—a means to have these leaders look at a church's style from an outsider's perspective. After meeting once a week for six weeks, these folks understood their own church's cornerstone, were grounded in kingdom themes, had a more personal relationship with Leith, and exhibited more attention to the principles of faithful church living. When I heard him, he had replicated this process eight times a year for six years and testified to the wonderful ripple effect it had produced in establishing a kingdom-centered cornerstone in that congregation.

A Quick Summary

The apostle Paul had a habit of birthing leadership communities—embedding the message and methods of Christ into a team of elders who were then empowered to carry on the work (Acts 14:23). In so doing, he accelerated the movement of the new church toward Jesus' missional agenda. When properly exercised, *leadership alignment* is a powerful means to encourage a church's core disciples to exchange their culturally based traditions for a biblically based community that prioritizes Jesus' disciple-making message and methods as defined by a shared cornerstone. When a church's leadership is aligned to common kingdom principles, the Spirit is given permission to accomplish more than humans can imagine.

The Discipline of Vision Casting

The first cornerstone discipline—*cornerstone discernment*—helps to secure Christ as the Head of the church, the starting point for forming a godly congregational culture. The second discipline—*leadership alignment*—further secures Jesus' rightful place by establishing an ongoing process that embeds and sustains disciple-making priorities within the core leaders of the church. The third cornerstone discipline—*vision casting*—completes this process by continually spreading this holy infection beyond the core leaders and into the entire community. In so doing, the congregation as a whole will increasingly realize the same spiritual transformation already experienced by the core: a turning away from self-serving, congregational habits and a renewed focus on Christ's missional agenda for His community. Once again, the biblical principle is clear: the more we collectively love and cooperate with what God wants to do in and through us, the more the Spirit's winds will be at our back (Jn. 14:15–17).

Back to the Future

Those who desire to see the church's God-inspired vision flourish within the church community should keep several foundational principles in mind.

First, the church needs and benefits from as many vision casters as possible. Unfortunately, many disciples falsely assume that vision casting is the sole purview of the "big dogs," or those few who possess a natural talent for public speaking. In fact, vision casting is simply a process for helping folks see, feel, and imagine a preferred future. As a result, any core disciple of the church can and should be a vision caster. It entails nothing more than enthusiastically sharing one's own perception of God's calling upon the church and the related benefits—the essence of the term "preferred." The more church members understand Jesus' desired destination and its benefits, the more likely they are to want to embrace the transformational journey and be participants. Note how often the Scriptures make reference to the benefits of faithfulness in both the Old and New Testaments. Any doubts? Just turn to the Book of Revelation and note the multiple sections that detail the rewards given to those who walk Jesus' path!

Second, no one, best way exists to cast the church's customized cornerstone and God-inspired vision. Limitless ways to do so can present themselves, and the best ways are always the ones that authentically resonate with a disciple's individual style and connect with the listener. Allow the practical strategies section below to spur your own thinking.

Third, churches should avoid vision casting to the congregation-at-large prior to clear progress in the first and second cornerstone disciplines—engaging in cornerstone discernment and forming a leadership community. I have learned this principle by observing more than a few pastors begin a culture transformation process through new member classes after his or her arrival. After several years of vision casting to the new folks, two distinct subcultures exist within the church: the long-standing members who are locked into the established culture, and the newer, enthusiastic participants who have bought into the pastor's personal cornerstone—one that lacks positional support. In other words, the "people of passion" are disconnected from the "people of position." This is a church with two incongruent cornerstones—one validated by time and the other validated by the new pastor—and is a bomb waiting for a fuse.

Finally, and most important, church leaders should be persistent. If you haven't gotten the message yet, hear me now: fostering the development of a kingdom culture is the heart of congregational discipleship and a never-ending task. Over and over again, the church's defined DNA must be embedded into the hearts and minds of participants. One of the central tasks of ambassadors, both paid and unpaid, is to keep the cornerstone in clear view and invite the congregation to be aligned to kingdom thinking. The bottom line is this: if the church's core disciples—most especially the pastor(s) and ministry staff—aren't tired of vision casting, they probably are not doing enough of it.

The Key Principles of Vision Casting

As a core leadership team meets together to design a vision casting strategy that promotes congregational discipleship, it needs to bear in mind these relevant principles:

- *Preach and Teach the Church's DNA:* Those in the pulpit should look for opportunities in preaching and teaching to challenge both "me" and "us" to take steps of faith. Much of the New Testament is written to you—second person plural, not singular, or, as we like to say in the South, "y'all." As Scripture passages lend themselves, preachers should remind listeners about the God-honoring vision and values that the church is seeking to realize through God's Spirit.

- *Leverage the Power of Technology:* Earlier this week, I stumbled onto a Web site from a Virginia church. The vision casting video embedded in its site was nothing short of brilliant. I was ready to pack up and move, it was so compelling. This church also had a virtual tour animation that effectively painted a picture of a prospective facility for the viewer. At Covenant, we are currently experimenting with vision casting specific ministries with brief recordings on CD's that include a quick summary of the heart of the ministry, testimonies from lay leaders, several anticipated questions along with answers, and a wrap-up invitation. We live in a wired world, and excellent vision casting must embrace the power of technology.

- *Memorize Key Biblical Passages:* Every God-inspired vision is biblically grounded with related key verses. Memorizing them allows vision casters to recite them verbatim when appropriate and helps to validate the transformational journey and its destination.

- *Utilize Biblical Stories that Model the Vision:* In similar fashion, church members should understand how their journey is paralleled in Scripture. Find and recite biblical stories whose purpose is to implant the elements of your vision into Christ's church.

- *Help Others Imagine the Future:* If folks are going to own and enthusiastically support the church's direction, they must be able to visualize the positive outcome of their contribution of time, resources, and energy. They must connect the picture of the relationship of their work to the realization of the vision. I often use the close of a meeting to vision cast the desired outcome of the group's efforts either through a brainstorming experience or through a time of prayer.

- *Help Servants Remember the Past:* Sometimes a look back enables lay servants to see the future more clearly. One example of this collective backward glance is when a church is approaching a facility expansion project. Encourage folks to consider how their church's foreparents paved the way for them and how their own time has arrived to create their own legacy for the generations to come.

- *Use the Example of Other Churches:* According to Myers-Briggs typology, 75 percent of the population primarily relies on their five senses to collect information about their world around them. (The others prefer their intuition—more of a gut instinct.) These "sensors" benefit from seeing a tangible example to visualize what they cannot see, touch, or smell. So show them! Take leaders to places where they can see a church that is farther down the path so they can experience what living into the vision will be like.

- *Use Examples from Church History:* For centuries, disciples have been faithful in living out the Gospel in their lives. What better way to see disciple-making in action than to read about the faithful of the past? Within the Methodist church I currently serve, we regularly make use of John Wesley and his ministry as an example of what we desire to become.

- *Affirm Your Church's Heroes:* As you birth a Christ-centered cornerstone, a handful of folks will start to embrace the DNA and, in turn, begin to model disciple-making leadership. Don't keep their actions and attitudes hidden under a basket. Let them be the salt and light that models to the rest of the community what faithfulness looks like.

- *Take Advantage of Any Story that Reflects Cornerstone Priorities:* The world is filled with fascinating people and events that often reinforce the God-inspired vision of the church. Be on the lookout for real life stories that provide a positive or negative example and further establish the need for the community's redemptive purpose.

- *Stimulate the Imagination in Prayer:* Though mentioned above, let me reinforce how prayer can be used to cast a vision. Our brains possess an enormous power to imagine what does not yet exist, a power that is seldom tapped. When people close their eyes to pray—especially at the end of a team meeting—help them imagine the outcome of their faithful service to Christ. Paint a mental picture that allows them to see in their minds' eye how life will be different and better because of their combined efforts. Better yet, get them to help you draw that picture and, in so doing, watch them come alive to more effectively playing their part.

- *Leverage Outside "Experts":* Hearing from those who have walked a similar path is always fun and encouraging. In our church, we use these kinds of outside experts to reinforce and validate the benefits of our congregation's vision and calling. And don't forget those ministry servants who are unable to attend for one reason or another—send them a recording so they stay in step with those present.

- *Walk the Talk as a Staff:* Vision casting is not the responsibility of the senior pastor alone. All core disciples need to be involved, but it won't happen without the staff's example. Just like the cornerstone itself, the staff must lead the way.

- *Tell Your Own Story:* Peter, a premiere ambassador, emphasizes the importance of our own stories: "*Always be prepared to give an answer to*

everyone who asks you to give the reason for the hope that you have" (1 Pet.
3:15). Sharing your passion for the vision Christ has given your
congregation speaks volumes, but you must be ready when the
opportunity arises.

- *Infiltrate Established Groups:* The vision casting methodologies outlined
above are all highly effective—and much more efficient—in a group
context. At Covenant, we are currently infiltrating our existing group
structure to vision cast the launching of a Saturday night service.
Our equipping staff are reinforcing our Great Commission motiva-
tion. Lay leaders are sharing testimonies. Handouts answer questions,
and CD's summarize the heart of the initiative. Our community
worship then becomes the icing on the cake where preaching calls
disciples to a new commitment. "Where two or three are gathered"
is a good place to share God's dreams!

The Transformation of Culture— When Can We Stop Vision Casting?

Remember my comments at the beginning of chapter 3? I described
how great it would be to arrive at our destination—godliness—through
the click of a mouse at www.discipleship.com. Obviously, I was just joking;
but you'd be surprised by how many people think that a church's culture
can change in a matter of months. If you are tempted to share this
perspective, consider this question: How long does it take a new Jesus
follower who has been living a self-serving lifestyle for decades to fully
embrace the Lord's servant-focused commands—assuming he or she
consistently commits his or her ways to God? When I pose this question,
the vast majority of people answer years. Why? Because they reflect on
their own lives and how long it has taken them individually to experience
Christ's transformational power. If experiencing a radical shift in priorities
takes years for folks like you or me, do you think the process of exchanging
a self-centered world for one in which Christ is at the center would be
any different or any quicker for a whole body of people, His local church?

Typically, significant and enduring cultural change within a local
church takes five to seven years. Obviously, this is a generalized truth.
No two churches are alike, and God can undoubtedly use spectacular
events to quickly reinvent His people. Normally, however, this transformational process is about hundreds of small steps of faith rather than a few
huge, paradigm-shifting leaps. So patience and persistence are necessary
ingredients in cultivating a church culture focused on Christ's mission in
the world. No shortcuts, magic wands, or wishful thinking can bring about
a cultural transformation. No substitute exists for the daily discipline of
vision casting built on a validated cornerstone and a related community

of core disciples. One need only look around at the examples of long-tenured pastors who know how to daily exercise these three disciplines—discerning a cornerstone, forming a leadership community, and casting a vision of the desired outcome. (John Ed Mathison, Bill Hybels, Leith Anderson, and Rick Warren are but a few that come to mind.) The legacy of their church's cultures speaks volumes.

A QUICK SUMMARY

At the very end of Jesus' time on earth, He stood among His most faithful followers and cast a compelling vision of a changed world: "[Y]ou will be my witnesses in Jerusalem, and in all Judea and Samaria, and to the ends of the earth" (Acts 1:8b). They got the message and obediently obeyed His teachings as evidenced by their amazing legacy of faith that you and I enjoy today. When properly exercised, *vision casting* is a powerful means to encourage the entire church to exchange its comfortable and self-fulfilling expectations for a lifestyle characterized by an urgent passion for the hurting and lost. If we love Christ, we collectively follow His Great Commission, disciple-making path; and the Spirit empowers every step of faith.

Emerging Truth about Congregational Discipleship

Once again, Jesus is the Master Teacher on the subject of congregational life. All we need to do is follow His lead. The three cornerstone disciplines outlined above are nothing more than the pattern He modeled for us—disciplines that keep God on the throne and His people aligned to kingdom priorities and collectively engaged in a transformational, discipleship process.

As we review what we have learned, a handful of principles will strengthen our understanding and capacity to provide insightful leadership:

- *Cultivating congregational faithfulness begins with a defined, Christ-centered cornerstone—the discipline of congregational discernment.* The discernment of congregational identity—as represented by articulated values, beliefs, vision, and mission—is rooted in prayer and His Word. Such congregational discernment helps secure Christ as the church's Head and keeps a church focused on His mission rather than its own agenda.
- *Keeping Christ King is founded upon an intentional community of ambassadors—the discipline of leadership alignment.* Jesus spent the vast majority of his limited three years in ministry developing a committed team of followers. Day after day, He embedded the kingdom's DNA into their souls. We see the rich rewards of His investment: a band

of followers willingly pouring out their lives for the Gospel.

- *Enabling the larger community to understand and embrace Christ's authority accelerates the transformation of congregational culture—the discipline of vision casting.* Even though Jesus mentored a small, handpicked group, He utilized numerous large-group events to describe a kingdom approach to life and the related benefits of faithfulness.

- *Practicing cornerstone disciplines is a never-ending process.* Just like their individual counterparts, congregational disciplines are daily activities that keep us engaged in an ongoing discipleship process: moving us farther and farther away from our worldly paradigms of church life, in which we are consumers, and closer and closer to a world in which all congregational disciples are ambassadors for Jesus Christ.

Assuming that your church's cornerstone is defined, embedded into a community of committed disciples, and embraced by the congregation, the hard part now begins. The next three ministry disciplines will show us how to flesh out cornerstone living in ways that honor the King.

DISCUSSION QUESTIONS

Cornerstone Discernment

1. Is your church aligned to a Christ-centered cornerstone? If so, does this cornerstone answer the foundational questions: *What is important (values)? What is essential (beliefs)? Where are we going (vision)?* and *How will we get there (mission)?*

2. What process was utilized to establish these defining statements? To what extent were these statements discerned rather than decided?

3. Is the cornerstone strongly linked to the Scriptures? To what extent does the church's DNA enjoy wide understanding and ownership?

4. Is the cornerstone and its vision up to date? If not, what is the best process for launching a discernment process? Who are some of the individuals who would be effective as planning team members?

Leadership Alignment

1. Is the church's staff modeling the cornerstone and setting the pace for lay leaders?

2. Assuming that a Christ-centered cornerstone is in place, how well has this DNA been embedded in the core leaders of the church—both the people of position *and* the people of passion?

3. Has there been an intentional effort to form a leadership community that owns the church's vision? How does the staff communicate and invest their lives in these leaders?

4. What are the most effective means for helping emerging leaders understand and embrace the church's cornerstone—making outsiders insiders? What organizational systems currently need to be realigned to the cornerstone?

Vision Casting

1. Is the DNA regularly reinforced in worship and verbally by the lead pastor?

2. How well are lay leaders vision casting the DNA? Are they being taught and challenged to do so?

3. Does a review of the church's communication systems—including all logos and symbols—show that the church's DNA is self-evident? Are the subministries in step with these cornerstone definitions?

4. How well does the community understand the church's core ideology? Does it grab their attention?

9

Ministry Disciplines

Establishing Christ's Disciple-Making Methods

> *"Therefore go and make disciples of all nations, baptizing them in the name of the Father and of the Son and of the Holy Spirit, and teaching them to obey everything I have commanded you."*
>
> JESUS (Mt. 28:19)

Talk is cheap. Anyone can brag about what he or she is going to do. Actually walking the talk—ruthlessly aligning one's life to stated goals and priorities—is not only rare, it's impressive. I have been a student of high achievers for the past thirty years, especially in the world of sports. I am fascinated by those who see their goals clearly, align their lives to achieve them, and go on to do just that. I have consumed a steady diet of biographies, books, magazine articles, and TV shows in my effort to understand why these types of people excel. In recent years, I have been caught up in the stories of superstars Lance Armstrong and Curt Schilling, but my curiosity with over-the-top athletic achievement actually began in 1972 with Dan Gable.

The name Dan Gable may not ring too many bells for you, but he is widely acclaimed as the greatest amateur wrestler in our country's history. During his prep and college careers, Gable compiled an unbelievable record of 182–1. He was undefeated in 64 prep matches and was 118–1 at Iowa State. His only defeat came in the NCAA finals his senior year. Gable was a three-time all-American and three-time Big Eight champion. He set NCAA records in winning and pin streaks. At the 1972 Summer Olympics he won a gold medal without surrendering a single point to any of his opponents who were not pinned in their match.[1] What makes overachievers like Gable tick? Besides enviable natural ability, words like *focused, relentless,* and *persistent* aptly describe champions' personalities and lifestyles. Obviously, the success of these stellar athletes is no accident

113

or fluke. Their success comes from years of unyielding results-oriented effort.

So it is with faithful churches. Congregations that obediently live into their Christ-centered cornerstones do so by being highly intentional and focused year after year. Dallas Willard makes a fascinating and parallel observation: "Any successful plan for spiritual formation, whether for the individual or group, will in fact be significantly similar to the Alcoholics Anonymous program."[2] His point is simple: sobriety does not happen by accident. A recovering alcoholic can pursue an addiction-free world only through the daily, intentional, and relentless exercise of discipline. Sounds like the style and pattern of great athletes, doesn't it? Herein lies the central purpose and role of ministry disciplines–to keep a church intentionally and relentlessly moving toward establishing the cornerstone ideals. Only this kind of single-minded pursuit will enable a church to achieve its full kingdom potential.

The Purpose of Ministry Disciplines

The discernment of a Christ-centered cornerstone is a powerful discipline that enables a congregation to accelerate the process of dying to self and living for Christ, but it's only the first step. In fact, more and more churches have some semblance of a cornerstone. Many have mission statements even though they frequently have an uncanny resemblance to larger, well-known churches and lack broad-based ownership or understanding. A statement of theological beliefs is also fairly common and is sometimes related to a church's denomination. Congregational value and vision statements that reflect the heart of God are rarer still. But what you almost never see is a cornerstone-based mission being put into action, which is why a church needs ministry disciplines. Such deliberate disciplines move the church closer to establishing Jesus' disciple-making methods as the norm for its ministry to adults, students, and children. The more it moves toward this end, the more it cooperates with God's redemptive power. In this chapter, I will outline three ministry disciplines: relevant worship, spiritual formation, and lay mobilization. When properly exercised, these disciplines keep congregations obediently moving towards Christ's priorities–"making disciples of all nations" (Mt. 28). All churches, though called to unique visions individually, share this common purpose of growing disciple-making disciples. As already mentioned, I have found Paul's three-pronged model of "invite...grow...send" as an understandable, transferable model for describing Christ's method. This three-pronged model is the basis for these three ministry disciplines.

Three Essential Ingredients: The Heart and Soul of Ministry Disciplines

Ministry disciplines focus on helping a congregation emulate Christ's *methods* as it articulates His *message*. This "invite...grow...send" method or process can only be realized, however, if several biblical values are firmly in place. Let's take a moment to touch on these essential priorities that lay a foundation for these powerful disciplines.

TEAMWORK—HOW WE SERVE TOGETHER IN MINISTRY

No doubt about it: The church is to function as a collegial community of faith. For Jesus' entire earthly ministry, He modeled intimate community with His disciples. Paul's imagery of a body in 1 Corinthians 12 is also crystal clear—all communities of faith are to function as teams. Additionally, Luke lifts up the Early Church (Acts 2:42–47) as a testimony to this truth, and the letters of the New Testament repeatedly implore readers to live together with a spirit of peace, harmony, and cooperation, even in the midst of diversity (Eph. 4:1–8). Regrettably, many churches adopt their group ministry methodologies from their secular surroundings and often fail to embrace this biblical priority. More on that later.

So, what does biblical teamwork look like? David Stark and Patrick Keifert insightfully highlight seven realities present when Christ-centered community exists:

1. *synergism* (1 Cor. 12:4–31): people are able to accomplish more when they combine their energies and talents than when they work alone
2. *support and belonging* (Eccl. 4:9–12): people enjoy a greater sense of belonging to a church community when others know them, affirm them, and support them
3. *accountability* (Jas. 5:19–20): people are able to make and stick to personal goals better when they have a support system helping them
4. *transformation* (1 Thess. 1:5–7): small groups empower people to make changes in their lives
5. *decision making and problem solving* (Prov. 15:22): groups of people generate higher quality decisions and solutions than individuals do alone
6. *risk taking and experimentation* (Ex. 4:1–7): people feel safer trying new things when they are in a supportive environment
7. *learning* (Josh. 1:8): within the context of a group, people retain more of the information they learn and remember it longer than they would if they learned it alone[3]

The more these attributes are present, the more the leadership of the church can be confident that authentic, Christian community is being realized. So, how does a church community function in step with these biblical ideals? How does a church embed them throughout all ministries? Four sequential steps are called for:

1. the church must clearly affirm the value of teamwork within its cornerstone
2. the church's paid staff must be growing toward these biblical ideals
3. a system must be adopted that puts these values firmly in place
4. team facilitators have to be trained continuously [4]

In my current setting, we use an adaptation of Cousins and Bugbee's acrostic model (C.O.S.T.) to remind ourselves of the key components of any ministry team (see appendix 3). *C* stands for *Calling,* the process of forming a team. It includes defining the team's vision and mission, identifying the related roles of its servants, and inviting gifted disciples to participate. *O* stands for *Orientation,* the process of initially building the team and insuring that relevant information, training, and relationship building occurs. *S* stands for *Sustaining,* the process of supporting the team as it moves toward its defined objectives and, in so doing, keeps servants appreciated, growing, and living into their kingdom potential. Last, *T* stands for *Transitioning,* the process for helping participants gracefully exit the ministry when appropriate, includes assessment, "carefrontation" when needed, and a referral process. The C.O.S.T. model ties right back to the Master's methods and how He desires His Church to operate. Teamwork that honors our spiritual gifts is an absolutely essential ingredient to the ministry disciplines *invite...grow...send,* and *means we serve together.*

SPIRITUAL GIFTS—HOW WE FIND OUR PLACE IN MINISTRY

In like fashion, Paul spelled out how the Spirit has uniquely gifted the people of God to build up the body of Christ (1 Cor. 12; Rom. 12; Eph. 4). Paul was quite concerned that the faith community might be uninformed about each member's "grace gifts": "Now about spiritual gifts, brothers, I do not want you to be ignorant" (1 Cor. 12:1). Yet here we stand almost two thousand years later, and many churches still fail to affirm or teach the basic truths in regards to this critical element. Rightly understood, spiritual gifts are "'*divine abilities distributed by the Holy Spirit*' (1 Cor. 12:11) '*to every believer according to God's design and grace*' (1 Pet. 4:10) 'for *the common good of the body of Christ*' (1 Cor. 12:7)."[5] As a result, linking a person's Spirit-inspired gifts to his or her role within ministry teams is another, nonnegotiable part of both Jesus' and Paul's method.

Unfortunately, confusion remains among many church leaders about the nature and purpose of spiritual gifts. Based on my experience, four common misperceptions about spiritual gifts plague the Church.

First, many confuse natural talents with spiritual gifts. Natural talents are given at our physical birth, whereas spiritual gifts are given at our spiritual birth. Though God gives both, only believers receive spiritual gifts.

Second, more than a few disciples confuse spiritual gifts with the fruits of the Spirit (Gal. 5:22, 23). The fruits of the Spirit are a natural by-product of an abiding and obedient relationship with Jesus Christ. The fruits of the Spirit are best understood as "being" qualities, while spiritual gifts are "doing" abilities. Both spiritual gifts and fruit of the Spirit are essential for effective ministry.

Third, some confuse spiritual gifts with spiritual disciplines. As we have already highlighted, spiritual disciplines primarily strengthen the individual disciple, while spiritual gifts primarily strengthen others.

Finally, some disciples confuse spiritual gifts with ministry positions. Ministry titles indicate general roles, while spiritual gifts indicate specific functions. In other words, ministry titles tend to indicate organizational position, whereas spiritual gifts indicate ministry contribution.

I grew up in a large, evangelical church, but did not discover my gifts from any training I received there. I went to an excellent seminary that I love, but did not discover them there either. Discovering my spiritual gifts also did not happen through seminars or spiritual gift inventories. Trust me on this one: *Ministry experience is the key to spiritual gift discovery.* So, here is my advice: buy an easy-to-understand book on the subject of spiritual gifts, read it through once, and jump into a ministry that you think you may like. After 6–12 months, go back to your book's listing of spiritual gifts and see what fits. I would also give this listing to those you have been serving with and ask for their counsel. The big lesson here is this: spiritual gifts are best discovered in ministry. This should come as no surprise, since Jesus trained folks *in* ministry, not *for* ministry. Using our spiritual gifts to serve God and His people is an absolutely essential ingredient in the ministry disciplines. *Invite…grow…send means we serve in a manner consistent with how God has wired us.*

Mentoring—How We Are Prepared in Ministry

In retrospect, we can now see that the Industrial Revolution had a huge impact on the discipleship strategies of Western churches. Up until that time, mentoring, or apprenticing, was the primary way in which more mature disciples passed on their knowledge and skills to younger believers. In the same way that parents "apprenticed" their children, seasoned disciplers used a four-step developmental process: *You watch me do a task; we do it together; I watch you do it; then you do it on your own.* A quick review of the gospels reveals that mentoring in this manner was Jesus' primary strategy for passing on to His core leaders the basics of both His message and method. The same strategy was successful for generations.

The onset of the Industrial Revolution however, created huge, rapid shifts in the Western world. As many adolescents chose to leave the farm and head toward the larger cities; and new, large-scale approaches to education were birthed to handle the masses. The reason? Parents were no longer able to train their children in the life skills that they would need to succeed in the emerging, urban marketplace. So began an enormous shift away from apprenticing and toward a formal classroom model of education. Today, this model of training not only continues to dominate the academic landscape, but is the preferred approach to discipleship among many Western churches.

To be sure, the classroom model of education has its merits in teaching a large group of people. However, to accomplish the Great Commission priorities—making disciple-making disciples—mentoring remains the preferred and most effective method. Thankfully, mentoring is making a comeback, and folks such as Stacy Rinehart are leading the way.[6] Stacy debunks a common myth by rightfully pointing out that biblical mentoring does not mean being "omni-competent" in every aspect of the Christian life and or ministry. Each believer has something to teach others in specific areas. These areas are places where disciples have learned important life lessons and are able to share the following with other disciples:

1. wisdom from experiences, a listening ear, and direction
2. encouragement, camaraderie, and friendship in times of struggles
3. personal development suggestions

Mentoring, when done correctly, motivates disciples to move ahead boldly, enables them to proceed with newfound wisdom, and increases their eagerness for being a part of an ongoing ministry. Indeed, nothing substitutes for being on the "playing field" with a guide who has relevant life experience. Jesus and Paul modeled this excellent method for us. Mentoring is an essential ingredient in the ministry disciplines. *Invite... grow...send means we apprentice other disciples in the life lessons we have learned along the way.* Teamwork, spiritual gifts, and mentoring are three ingredients essential to Jesus' process of disciple-making, *and* to the three related ministry disciplines we will soon look at. But first, let me tell you the "sugar story."

I greatly admire my wife's wonderful cooking. Those who have been in our home know she is an awesome cook. As I tell you about this one, isolated gaff, you have to put it into the context of years of incredible dishes, especially sugar-based treats. Anyway, a few years ago, Mary Lou, our three boys, and I sat down to enjoy one of her outstanding Thanksgiving meals—the whole works from juicy turkey to Waldorf salad to her killer homemade crescent rolls. But the best was yet to come: her cherished pumpkin pie with a mouthwatering from-scratch crust, topped with whipped cream. As we all got our pieces of pie and launched mega-bites into our mouths, our taste buds jumped for joy with expectation. Within milliseconds, each set of eyes around the table bulged with surprise. What we had joyfully expected failed to be a reality. Instead of perfection, we tasted absolutely bland pumpkin pie. It looked perfect, but she had forgotten one ingredient: sugar. Trust me, pumpkin pie without sugar does not taste good. In fact, it's woeful! So what's the point? First, Mary Lou will never do that again! But, more importantly, trying to do ministry without honoring the biblical principles of teamwork, spiritual gifts, and mentoring is like eating pumpkin pie without sugar. Trust me—it's not good. It's not even mediocre; it's woeful! So, with the sweet taste of these three essential ingredients on your ministry palate, let's unpack the ministry disciplines one at a time.

The Discipline of Relevant Worship

The first step in Paul's (and Jesus') three-point method was proclamation: *inviting* listeners to let go of their world and embrace the Creator's. Paul's explanation of God's grace and forgiveness was relevant and life-changing because he delivered it at the audience's level and spoke in their terms. Acts 17 reveals this reality clearly through Paul's back-to-back presentations. Initially, Paul presented the Gospel to a Jewish audience. Predictably he relied on the Old Testament to make his case and key points. With his next audience—the Greeks—he radically shifted his tactics, supporting his arguments with their own philosophic assumptions and particular language.

In today's world, congregational worship represents the most common setting for extending this same kind of relevant invitation to those both inside and outside the church community. The first ministry discipline, *relevant worship,* translates a timeless Gospel into the audience's language, metaphors, and images. So why is relevant worship a helpful discipline in keeping a congregation obediently moving toward Christ-centeredness? Do you remember my explanation of "hire…watch…pay" in chapter 6, along with Bill Hull's "inviting" metaphor of a hospital?

Relevant worship is like other congregational disciplines in that it encourages us to collectively die to our "clubish" preferences and live for Christ's mission. All faith communities are tempted to turn their backs on the "sick" people beyond their walls—people who are broken and need a loving "hospital" in which they can recover from the bumps and bruises of life. Many congregations silently affirm that "we have enough members" and fail to be attentive to the needs of outsiders. The day a church shuts its "hospital door" is the day that church risks forfeiting its identity—one of the key reasons why a kingdom-focused cornerstone and this discipline of relevant worship are so important.

If you question the reality of Christian churches tending to ignore the spiritually lost, I again encourage you to read Alan Klaas's book *In Search of the Unchurched.* The findings reinforce the vital role of relevant worship. The researchers found that those churches that prioritized inviting the spiritually lost to exchange their world for Christ's (the Great Commission) were growing, and those that did not were not. The discipline of relevant worship helps to keep Christ enthroned as King by keeping the doors of the church open to those who are sick and desperately need to discover hope. It is the starting place for establishing a Great Commission mind-set.

Perhaps the idea of public worship being a welcoming and relevant place for both established disciples and those who are still seeking a relationship with God will be troubling for some. At least as far back as John Calvin, Christian leaders have recognized that public services blend both believers and unbelievers. Wasn't this the same reality and context when Jesus preached in a public setting? I cannot think of a more appropriate place for the lost to "catch" Christianity than being with disciples who are basking in God's presence. I am convinced so many unbelievers flocked to Jesus because they could see His intimacy with the Father.

The Key Principles of Relevant Worship

As a core leadership team meets together to design a relevant worship strategy that promotes congregational discipleship, it needs to bear in mind these principles:

- *Honor the Church's Cornerstone:* First and foremost, a leadership team must keep in step with what the church has discerned as its God-inspired vision and its target audience. "Relevance" always has to be discerned in light of the church's culture and its emerging direction. The worship leaders must constantly ask themselves two questions: *Whom has God called our church to reach?* and *What are the best worship and communication strategies to connect with this audience?* Like Paul, we should be eager to be understood and shape our presentation based on our intended audience. "To the weak I became weak, to win the weak. I have become all things to all men so that by all possible means I might save some" (1 Cor. 9:22).

- *Establish a Worship Planning Team:* A team of disciples that uses its diverse gifts to keep worship relevant, not only for those within the walls, but also those who are guests, is absolutely necessary. Equally important is a capable team leader. (Assume this "team-based" principle for all future disciplines!)

- *Keep in Touch with What Is Relevant:* "Relevance" is a moving target. As new generations emerge, tastes and preferred styles of music gradually evolve. As a result, worship teams have to constantly explore and reflect on what "works" within the church's surrounding community context. I highly encourage worship teams to attend conferences that challenge our human tendency to be stylistically static and myopic. Having a few younger adults on the team is also helpful!

- *Multi-track as Needed:* As congregations grow, they often arrive at a place where they benefit from a multi-track approach to worship. Establishing multiple worship services, with each one targeting a different audience can be an effective strategy. The most common model includes a "traditional" and "contemporary" choice. The traditional style will reflect a longer-standing and much-loved flavor of worship, while the contemporary will be more relevant to a younger target audience—presumably an emerging generation of believers. Remember: today's contemporary styles are tomorrow's traditions.

- *Minimize a Blended Approach:* Combining multiple styles within one service can be helpful on a seasonal basis, or when launching a new service. This approach, however, is seldom a wise, long-term strategy. It tends to frustrate many who have a clear, stylistic preference.

- *Plan Well in Advance:* Excellence takes time, and Christ deserves our best. The team—and especially the lead preacher(s)—will need to set aside a block of time periodically to draft worship themes that are months down the road. Then, as those dates get closer, the team can refine these concepts and all related components of worship.

- *Be Prepared to Add Another Service:* When the attendance at your "prime time" weekend services regularly exceeds 80 percent of capacity, it is time to begin planning another service or add space—or both.

Each strategy has its own unique issues, but Jesus' outreach-focused mission is a constant common denominator. Since He is King, our response has to be, "Whatever it takes!" A church's faithful obedience to "keep the doors open" becomes a source of renewal for that body of believers.

- *Match Outside Presenters to the Culture:* Outside preachers and speakers who were effective ten and twenty years ago may not be as relevant to audiences as they once were, especially if the church's vision or audience has changed. Alignment to the church's cornerstone should always be a primary issue when planning teams are considering invitations to outside presenters.

- *Be Intentional about Hospitality:* If the church wants to be an "inviting" place in which outsiders feel like insiders, related teams that champion hospitality to guests must be in place. To get a better feel for the importance of this ministry, send a handful of your folks to visit some other churches in your area. When they get back together, they can share experiences and discuss how it felt to be visitors, how they were treated, and what they learned. This group will be brimming with new insights on how your congregation can be more welcoming to guests.

- *Orient New Guests to the Church's Culture:* How will your church's guests discover your congregation's heart for Christ's mission? In my current congregation, our strategy is an experience we call "Icebreaker." Held about ten times a year, its vision is for newcomers to *"walk away...with a deep conviction that their walk with God matters, a clear understanding of Covenant's God-centered vision, and a desire to take their next, daring step of faith."* By design, Icebreaker focuses on answering three basic questions: Why does the church exist? What does it believe? and, Where is it going? This event is attended by Covenant "swarmers"–friendly, outgoing participants who help these newcomers feel welcome and encourage them to find their place within the church. (More on this process shortly.)

- *Stay in Touch with Related Facility Issues:* To stay open to outside guests, the leadership of the church will have to manage much more than worship styles. What is the parking situation for guests? Can the nursery handle more children with quality and ease so that visiting moms can worship with peace of mind? Does signage make it easy to find one's way? Are there people easily accessible to answer questions? Finally, can folks get in and out of the church easily? All of these factors influence the degree to which newcomers hear the message clearly and come back for more.

A Word about Music Style

Congregations don't have to wade too far into the topic of music styles before they hit the rough waters of contention—the fourth dimension of discipleship! Based on my own experience as well as conversations with Third World missionaries, music style in worship is a common focal point for heated disagreement everywhere. Music styles can be an equal-opportunity irritant! More often than not, a church struggles with these issues because it has no real clarity regarding its identity—it does not have a clear, comprehensive cornerstone. With no foundational DNA to direct the congregation's discernment, participants fill the vacuum with their own biases. Predictably, those who are used to a clubhouse atmosphere desire a worship style that reflects their own preferences. Those who view the church's mission as reaching the world for Christ— a hospital mentality—are more willing to provide worship services that are also relevant to the outside, unchurched community.

Can you feel the friction yet? Obviously these two camps of thought can quickly polarize and cripple a church community. When I find myself in the middle of these heated discussions, I encourage congregations to call a time out from their worship debates and focus on their kingdom cornerstone. In so doing, they will address the systemic issues—what they believe about God, why they exist as a community of faith, and where they discern God is calling them to go. I cannot stress enough the importance of having a widely shared church cornerstone! Once in place, the cornerstone greatly narrows the scope of debate and significantly decreases contention within faith communities.

We return to the hospital metaphor to grasp the importance of relevant worship. Such worship provides an intentional space and time in which those who need to experience God's healing touch and presence can do so. Obviously, no one music style is "right." This truth only serves to reinforce why having a unique, God-inspired vision is so important. Even the largest congregations cannot be all things to all people. They must discern whom they are being called to reach with the Gospel and tailor their worship offerings accordingly. Even churches of modest size are finding a multi-track approach that allows for choices in music styles a preferred strategy. Rather than limit themselves to one worship style, these churches provide choices for different people at different times.

A Quick Summary

I don't think I can ever overstate the importance of relevant worship that brings hurting people to the reality that Jesus Christ is Lord and King. This experience of the holy allows me to grasp more fully an astounding truth: God loved me so much that Jesus "did not consider equality with God something to be grasped, but made himself nothing, taking the very nature of a servant, being made in human likeness" (Phil. 2:6–7). That's relevance–face-to-face with the Creator who lived in my world. God put on skin and bones for me!

When properly exercised, the discipline of *relevant worship* is a powerful means to encourage a church to exchange its preoccupation with aging forms for an approach that effectively communicates a timeless Gospel to those in and beyond its walls. The resulting environment sets the stage for the movement of God's Spirit that can be felt and sensed by the invited guests of regular participants. And it leaves them hungry for more.

The Discipline of Spiritual Formation

As a nucleus of committed converts emerged, Paul moved on to the second step in the church-birthing process: *growing* followers of Christ. He accomplished this through mentoring, extended visits, messengers, and targeted letters to the faithful. Today, this focus is commonly referred to as *spiritual formation*. As Hull's greenhouse metaphor would suggest, this discipline seeks to firmly root both individual disciples and the church as a whole in God's Word and establish it as a foundation for life (Col. 2:6–7). Why is spiritual formation a helpful discipline in keeping a congregation obediently moving toward Christ-centeredness? This discipline–the second part of Paul's and Jesus' methodology–parallels all other congregational disciplines by encouraging us to exchange our culture's norms for God's ways. Here is but one example.

The vast majority of North American churches and their leadership teams use voting as a primary process for determining future action steps. This shouldn't come as a surprise to anyone since these congregations live within a democratic society. However, churches who adopt a democratic model of decision-making do so at their own peril since voting has no biblical precedent. When a church seriously pursues an understanding of the Scriptures–the discipline of spiritual formation–congregational leaders predictably begin to see the contrasts between its established ways and God's prescription for His Church. (Democracies reinforce humanity's reign, whereas a monarchy affirms the King's reign.) The goal of this congregational discipline, therefore, is to move us closer and closer to Christ's methodology as spelled out in the Word. I will address the issue of voting more in depth in the next chapter.

As with every other discipline, a church's spiritual formation process needs to be linked to a well-defined cornerstone. Once in place, the ministry disciplines–especially spiritual formation–take these shared biblical truths and drive them deeply into the hearts and minds of the people. As the church increasingly embraces and establishes these biblical standards as norms, the church's culture is transformed just as Jesus intended: we become the "light of the world"—a beacon of hope to the surrounding community.

The Key Principles of Spiritual Formation

As a core leadership team meets together to design a spiritual formation strategy that promotes congregational discipleship, it needs to bear in mind these relevant principles:

- *Remember that the Holy Spirit Is in Control:* As Paul points out: "I planted the seed, Apollos watered it, but God made it grow" (1 Cor. 3:6). Spiritual formation is ultimately God's job; the Church is just establishing opportunities for folks to get His Word planted in their hearts and be watered by supportive relationships with other disciples. Men and women are not and never will be in control. In the midst of human chaos, the Spirit makes all things new.
- *Be Attentive to Adult Learning Styles:* It is so easy—and tempting—to believe that everyone thinks and learns like you do. In the early years of professional ministry, I couldn't understand why others did not learn just like me—reading and reflecting on the written word. Thankfully, I began to see that I had to adopt relevant strategies such as drawing pictures and charts or using music and videos in my teaching. Over time, I saw that my presentations were more effective as I tapped into the learning styles of my listeners. Jesus Himself was a brilliant teacher who modeled this approach as He used various means to make His points. Fortunately, the number of quality videos, CD's, skits, workbooks, and literature is expanding rapidly. Prioritize keeping in touch with the emerging options.
- *Establish a Discipling Process for New Participants:* At Covenant, we subdivide adult discipleship—spiritual formation—into four themes, or what we call "transformational environments": (1) *Discovery*—finding new life in Christ; (2) *Belonging*—living in community; (3) *Understanding*—learning God's plan; (4) *Service*—partnering with God. To help new people get connected, we have an orientation strategy called "First Steps." (This is a follow-up to the "Icebreaker" strategy discussed in the prior discipline.) In this multi-week experience, participants are organized in table groups and have a facilitating "crew leader." Ideally, the crew leaders stay connected with these new folks until they get embedded into one of the transformational environments. As you can see, getting folks connected is an important priority for us.

- *Establish Core Orientation Events:* In keeping with our fourfold discipleship paradigm at Covenant, we have crafted core orientation events for each transformational environment that moves beyond First Step's one-session introduction. These practical learning opportunities enable participants to more fully understand a specific area of ministry. (These opportunities are somewhat analogous to Saddleback's core classes, but are developmental in nature—not sequential.) Our goal is simply to get folks connected to their next step of faith.
- *Balance Classroom and Small-Group Strategies:* As a congregation grows, its spiritual formation choices will likewise expand. As this process unfolds, those overseeing the development of the spiritual formation strategy are well advised to balance classroom and small-group offerings. The primary goal of the classroom model is correct thinking and tends to emphasize an up-front teacher. In contrast, the goal of a small-group strategy is primarily correct living and tends to emphasize dialogue and self-discovery. Both are of value, as I will expand on shortly.
- *Adopt a Multidimensional Approach to Small-Group Ministry:* When it comes to small-group ministry, one size does not fit all. Four distinct types exist, namely (1) relationship-building groups that focus on belonging, (2) learning groups that focus on understanding, (3) caring groups that focus on support, and (4) serving groups that focus on the accomplishment of a task.[7] Obviously, all ministry teams or groups include all four of these themes, but in varied proportions. One of the great benefits of embracing an integrated model and training approach is its ability to establish a "group language" for the church. Accordingly, all group leaders get schooled in the "101" basics of group life prior to their specialization in one of the four themes. So wherever these servants end up in the church, everyone is talking the same language. (As you have probably figured out already, group leaders gravitate to the kind of group that reflects their gifting.)
- *Prioritize a Mentoring Process of Leader Development:* Seasoned Bible teachers and small-group leaders do not grow on trees. They are a product of intentionality, time investment, and personal discipleship. Accordingly, don't let any opportunity slip for currently trained leaders to apprentice emerging contributors. One of my biggest regrets in ministry is that I did not learn this principle earlier, and so I missed numerous opportunities to let people learn with me.
- *Distinguish Between Theological Essentials and Nonessentials:* One of my mentors, Bob Tuttle Jr., encourages his students to understand the difference between essential and nonessential doctrines. His point:

some beliefs are essential and nonnegotiable truths. In your church, these are the ones that should be clearly affirmed by your cornerstone statement of beliefs. They should be held to firmly by all teaching leaders, and all learning opportunities should be aligned to them. On the other hand, many other areas of the Scriptures and related doctrines should be understood to be nonessential. These are those gray areas of God's Word, in which your congregation is comfortable with a multiplicity of perspectives. Obviously, all teaching leaders within the church necessarily need to affirm the essentials while at the same time being tolerant of the nonessentials—a practice that will help to mitigate theological contention.

- *Affirm Kindred, Community-Based Options:* In most communities, excellent discipleship opportunities abound outside the local church. Rather than being threatened by them, churches should affirm these choices if they are helping disciples learn the Bible and live faithful lives. At the same time, churches should counsel these same disciples to be discriminating listeners and to distinguish the essentials from the nonessentials as defined by the church's cornerstone beliefs.

Models of Learning

Over the last few centuries the Church in North America has tended to emphasize a classroom model in its discipleship of adults. The Sunday morning classroom model that emerged in the 1900s is a perfect example. Though effective at transferring head knowledge and Christian dogma, this learning model has proven less effective in encouraging heart transformation. It seems clear that even though Jesus regularly taught in a large-group setting, His primary approach to embedding His truth in others was small groups.

By biblical standards, I would define small groups as: (1) communities of disciples who regularly gather together for the purpose of growing in Christ, (2) rarely exceed 12 participants and (3) combine the four basic elements detailed above—relationship building, learning, caring, and mission. (Based on my experience, I include dyads [2] and triads [3] in this model since they enjoy many of the same benefits as groups with 5–12 participants.) The benefits to a small-group approach to spiritual formation are fivefold.

First, small-group ministry broadens the pool of potential leaders since it is not dependent upon a seasoned teacher. Almost anyone can effectively provide group leadership.

Second, small groups are more adaptable to the multiplicity of schedules in today's busy world. Groups can meet whenever and wherever the participants choose.

Third, a small group provides its participants with personal relationships, prayer, and accountability. These ingredients are essential to life transformation and further underscore the benefits of group-based discipleship.

Fourth, small groups easily accommodate themselves to the needs and competencies of the participants. A classroom model is not nearly as adaptable and cannot easily address unique niches.

Finally, small groups more effectively inspire personal transformation. Classrooms tend to reach my head, while small groups shape my heart. It's the approach Jesus prioritized as He trained and led His own followers.

Quick Summary

Spiritual formation is nothing more than the process of realigning our secularized hearts and minds to the Doctor's written prescription for abundant life. In so doing, we arrive at His desired destination as we collectively realize this truth: "Do not conform any longer to the pattern of this world, but be transformed by the renewing of your mind. Then you will be able to test and approve what God's will is—his good, pleasing and perfect will" (Rom. 12:2).

Accordingly, when properly exercised, the discipline of *spiritual formation* is a powerful means to encourage a church to exchange its own notions of truth for a world in which the God-inspired Scriptures are the manual for daily living. As the church collectively complies with the commands of Christ, God honors this faithful obedience by sending the Spirit to be present, to show the way, and to empower the journey.

The Discipline of Lay Mobilization

The third step in both Jesus' and Paul's kingdom-expansion methodology—*sending*—empowered disciples to be God's ambassadors. Paul trained those who faithfully responded and then commissioned them by leaving the ministry in their hands (Acts 20:13–38). In like fashion, Jesus blessed His post-resurrection community, promised power and gifts from on high, and commissioned them to go to the "ends of the earth" (Acts 1:1–8). Increasingly, churches call this empowering process *lay mobilization*—launching equipped disciples to be fulfilled and effective in their service to Christ (Eph. 4:1–16). Why is lay mobilization a helpful discipline in keeping a congregation obediently moving toward establishing a Christ-centered ministry? This discipline is the third part of Paul's—and Jesus'—method and encourages church leaders, as well as all participants, to reject consumer-based approaches to ministry. I am convinced, however, that the vast majority of church staff and laypeople really don't want this lay mobilization exchange process to occur. Let me explain.

As a current staff member, I really do like the "hire…watch…pay" method of doing ministry, which is the opposite of lay mobilization. It strokes my ego. It keeps me in the spotlight. It affirms me as omni-competent. It makes the church dependent on my contribution. It feeds my insecurities. It plays into all my dysfunctions![8] As a layperson, I also like "hire…watch…pay," but for very different reasons. I love to be the object of the staff's personal attention when I need care rather than settling for aid from one of my peers–a lay minister. I love my discretionary time and would prefer to not use it to serve the world's needs. My time is more valuable to me than my money. I love to avoid getting my hands dirty with the missional tasks of Jesus. I love to dodge uncomfortable situations in which I am confronted by pain, illness, and poverty. I love to side-step settings in which I have to live sacrificially and share my resources with others. I love to play dumb so I can avoid having to learn how to contribute my spiritual gifts to the building of God's kingdom.

Fortunately, a growing number of congregations are rejecting hire…watch…pay and recapturing the true meaning of the "priesthood of all believers"–the Reformation's term for lay mobilization. It's about time, don't you think? Even Paul was concerned about the lack of awareness among the Early Church's disciples: "Now about spiritual gifts, brothers, I do not want you to be ignorant" (1 Cor. 12:1). But here we are, almost two thousand years down the road, and most congregations still struggle with this biblical mandate. The reason? The discipline of lay mobilization, like all congregational disciplines, is a spiritual issue. To be a faithful community of Christ, a church has to replace the values of "me"-centered consumerism and complacency with the values of Christ-centered servanthood and missional action. Once again, the heart of congregational discipleship comes down to the basic issue of kingship.

The Key Principles of Lay Mobilization

As a core leadership team meets together to design a lay mobilization strategy that promotes congregational discipleship, it needs to bear in mind these relevant principles:

- *Lay the Right Foundation:* The value of lay-empowered ministry must be clearly stated in your cornerstone and widely owned by the church's leadership before you launch this discipline. The flower of lay mobilization will only bloom when the church's soil (culture) has the proper nutrients. Until the biblical priority of lay ministry is in place and affirmed as Jesus' preferred way, no church will be able to implement successfully a comprehensive mobilization strategy. Lay ministry will only endure and thrive in a church that has identified the empowerment of laity as a method of the King.

- *Focus on Implementing Values, not Models:* A variety of effective mobilization models have emerged in recent years to help congregations establish this important process of empowerment. However, don't be deceived: lay mobilization is not a program but a mindset with a related set of biblical values. The model the church utilizes is simply a means to an end. Continually emphasize and teach the church's Bible-based cornerstone themes.[9]
- *Establish Empowerment from the Top Down:* Like everything else, the staff and core leadership have to be aligned to these values and model them before they will take hold throughout the congregation.
- *Install a Point Person:* A common thread among churches that have lived into these values is the existence of a point person. The point person sees the big picture of all the ministries and can visualize the who, when, and how of lay mobilization for the entire church. Such a coordinator, paid or unpaid, is essential.
- *Develop a Customized and Dynamic Process:* The process for equipping and launching laity into ministry needs to reflect the size and complexity of a church's context. In a smaller setting, the process can be very informal and rely on a skilled interviewer who knows all the people as well as all the opportunities. Larger congregations have to construct much more complex systems to coordinate their servants. Additionally, be prepared to flex with the growth of the church and the needs of the ministries.
- *Allow Passion to Drive Mobilization:* My early efforts in this ministry area were focused on helping people discover their spiritual gifts and using this information to help them find their place in ministry. I learned, though, that most people are clueless about spiritual gifts. I have since discovered that servants can more easily discern their "passion"–the one overwhelming desire they have for a particular ministry. By God's design, each of us has been given a piece of his heart, an area of ministry that we are passionate about. Some are passionate for kids; others are passionate for the lost; still others are passionate for the poor. My recommendation is to help people find their place in ministry via passion through either a classroom setting, a mentoring relationship, and or a service experience. Once they arrive in the right ministry area, then they can more easily discover their gifting as needed through ministry experience combined with the affirmation of others.[10]

- *Be Prepared to Decentralize the Process as the Church Grows:* With growth, a time comes when the church is best served by decentralizing the process because it has grown beyond one person. When this occurs, you will be very glad that the church is "passion-driven" because folks can easily be referred to an area of ministry and be greeted by an embedded "ministry connector" who focuses within that specific area. These ministry connectors are mobilizers who know all the ins and outs of the ministry and serve as "air traffic controllers" for all those who are coming and going in the ministry. (At Covenant, these paid and unpaid servants are well trained in the C.O.S.T. system and pay special attention to orientation and transitional needs of servants.) These connectors are also linked to other connectors throughout the church so they can easily refer folks who are transitioning to new places in ministry.

- *Distinguish between a Unique and a Community Contribution:* Like the other disciplines, lay mobilization has its own distinctive jargon and language. "Community contribution" has proven helpful in my ministry. Lay mobilization focuses on helping people find their niche in building Christ's kingdom—that place through which their gifting and passion can be leveraged through the power of God. But at other times a community contribution is needed. For instance, if another hurricane hits our North Carolina coast and six inches of silt gets dumped in our church basement, I am not going to be seeking servants who have a special passion and gifting for silt removal. My goal? To find folks who have strong backs and shovels! Everyone needs to pitch in at times to get critical goals accomplished—a community contribution. This principle is particularly relevant for portions of children's ministry!

- *Be on the Lookout for Emerging Ambassadors:* The second cornerstone discipline—leadership alignment—detailed a number of principles related to building a leadership community aligned to the church's DNA. New prospects for this essential community emerge in the lay mobilization process. As folks discover and align themselves to their passion and spiritual gifts, they are naturally—and should be intentionally—invited to be a part of the church's core community.

From Service-based to Servant-based

Lately, I have been learning a great deal from Don Cousins. One of the four original staff leaders, Don served at Willow Creek Community Church outside Chicago for 17 years.[11] For more than a decade, he has refined his understanding of biblical faithfulness as a congregational coach.

One of Don's key convictions is that a church needs to be *servant-focused* rather *service-focused.* I agree with Don's assertion that the vast majority of North American evangelical churches are primarily focused on the task of ministry—a service mindset. He argues, however, that this runs counter to the model of Jesus, who prioritized raising up empowered servants.

First, for the vast majority of their time with Jesus, the disciples saw themselves as the end product—not as a means to an end. At the Trans-figuration (Mt. 17), Peter, James, and John were ready to set up shop permanently, oblivious to a mission beyond themselves. Jesus did not clarify the mission until the very end of His time with them.

Second, Jesus did not focus on serving the masses, but on equipping a handful of servants—the three just mentioned, the 12 Apostles, the 72 disciples, and the 120 followers.

Third, He focused on their development more than on their ministry results. He sent the 72 out in pairs (Lk. 10). As they returned, Jesus focused not so much on what they accomplished, but on what they learned and experienced.

Fourth, Jesus was quick to restore Peter even in the face of ministry failure, another sign that Jesus was more concerned about growing people than growing ministry.

Finally, even Jesus' Heavenly Father modeled this reality. When was Jesus affirmed as a valued person—after He had accomplished His calling or before? The answer: before—at His baptism in the Jordan prior to His ministry's launching (Mt. 3). If we are to emulate Jesus' methods, our goal should be to grow leaders through ministry rather than grow ministry through leaders. Servant-focused or service-focused? The King seems to have a preference!

A Quick Summary

Whether we like it or not, the Church of Jesus Christ is not called to be a cruise ship where members are pampered by staff who meet their every whim. The Church is called to be an icebreaker—a ship on a life-and-death mission. Now you know why Covenant's orientation is called "Icebreaker"! When properly exercised, *lay mobilization* is a powerful means to encourage a church to exchange its consumer-driven expectation to be nurtured by the staff for a humble desire to be an instrument of change destined to make an eternal difference. With submission to a God-inspired vision for service to the world, active participants experience the Spirit's power moving in and through them to accomplish more for the kingdom than they could ever have imagined.

Emerging Truths about Congregational Spiritual Disciplines

Isaiah points out that God's ways are very different from our ways. So it is no surprise that the twenty-first–century church tends to distort the biblical model to fit its own worldly culture. In the process, disciple making gets derailed. Today, many churches have a fourfold strategy. First, attract a crowd. Use excellent oratory, snappy music, and programs for kids to entice the masses to show up on the church's doorstep. (All are worthy strategies within the right context.) Next, work to get these folks to live in Christian community using a small-group model. Third, hope and trust that the power of the Holy Spirit shows up. Finally, pray that all the pieces somehow fall into place and the church's membership grows.

Instead, let me suggest the reverse order—a biblical sequence for ministry.

First, make obediently waiting upon the Lord the top priority (Acts 1:4–14). A time of listening and learning and praying is the heart of cornerstone discernment.

Next, rejoice in the arrival of the Holy Spirit (Acts 2:1–4). As Jesus promised, the Spirit arrives on the heels of faithful obedience (Jn. 14:15–17).

Third, cooperate with the Spirit's work by faithfully embracing the time-tested methods for disciple making (Acts 2:42–46). In so doing, an authentic Christian community naturally emerges, one that is highly attractive to outsiders.

As this occurs, evangelism emerges as the fourth stage and a natural by-product of a Spirit-infused community. In other words, as visitors see the presence and power of God within His people, they become hungry for more. Their hearing and understanding of the Good News becomes a simple task (Acts 2:47). Once again, the choice boils down to doing things our way or bowing to God's way. Which do you think has a more lasting impact?

As we review what we have learned, a handful of principles will strengthen our understanding and capacity to provide effective leadership:

* *Establishing the King's ways begins with extending an irresistible invitation— the discipline of relevant worship.* An understandable proclamation of the Good News was Jesus' and Paul's starting point for making disciples who make disciples. As congregations emulate this pattern, they strive for external relevance and prioritize Jesus' command to "make disciples of all nations." In so doing, they keep moving toward

becoming a Christ-centered community and achieving their full kingdom potential.

- *Jesus' methods are further reinforced as the congregation embraces a biblical foundation for community life—the discipline of spiritual formation.* As congregations become more biblically literate, they are able to increasingly let go of approaches to life that mirror their surrounding culture. In so doing, they realign their lives and community to both the message of hope and the method by which this hope is to be taken to "the ends of the earth."

- *The reign of Christ is further established as servants are empowered to contribute in situations in which they are faithful, fruitful, and fulfilled—the discipline of lay mobilization.* How tempting it is to live on a cruise ship where passengers are coddled and the crew are tipped for their service, but that is not the King's design. Jesus' ways call for all hands on deck, with everyone having their place based on how He has wired them. And as a church exchanges its tendency for "hire...watch...pay" for "invite...grow...send," the power and presence of God's Spirit is increasingly felt and witnessed. As promised, God and His Spirit are attracted to faithful obedience!

Cornerstone disciplines secure the crown on Jesus' head. Ministry disciplines establish the King's ways as the norm. In the next chapter, we will see how support disciplines supply faithful servants with the resources they need to sustain kingdom building.

DISCUSSION QUESTIONS

Relevant Worship

1. To whom is the current worship relevant? If there are multiple services, are there distinctive differences among them? To what degree is this style(s) relevant for the unchurched community within a five–mile radius?

2. Does the church's cornerstone define any target audience? If so, how is this being reflected in the worship strategy and style? If not, what does the present worship style suggest about the current target audience?

3. Do the current worship attendance and the church's vision suggest a new worship service needs to be launched within the next few years? To what audience would this be new initiative be directed?

4. Is there a worship arts team in place? Are there complimentary teams in place to oversee hospitality and guest follow up? What systems, signage, and practices are in place to make outsiders feel like insiders? Is the facility–especially the nursery–accommodating to newcomers?

Spiritual Formation

1. What is the church's current spiritual formation strategy? What are the staff and lay leaders modeling?

2. How does the church intentionally develop group and teaching leaders? How is their training being linked to the cornerstone bedrock beliefs?

3. Is there a balanced combination of classroom and small group offerings? What are the core learning objectives and offerings for disciples? How are newcomers linked to their "next step of faith"?

4. What model of small-group ministry is most effective within your church's context? What is the process for forming and launching new small groups? How are newcomers assimilated into groups?

Lay Mobilization

1. How is the value of lay ministry defined within cornerstone statements? To what extent are these being understood and owned by the congregation?

2. Is there a point person who oversees lay mobilization? What communication systems do they utilize to keep track of people and needs?

3. How is staff trained to equip and organize emerging servants? Is empowering laity in ministry a primary responsibility and value of the staff? How is their effectiveness measured?

4. Are disciples being trained for or in ministry? Are their ministry roles and related expectations clearly defined?

10

Support Disciplines

Sustaining Christ's Mission and People

> *Go to the ant, you sluggard;*
> *consider its ways and be wise!*
> *It has no commander,*
> *no overseer or ruler,*
> *yet it stores its provisions in summer*
> *and gathers its food at harvest.*

SOLOMON (Prov. 6:6–8)

Consider termites. Individually, they have little intelligence. Yet collectively they build mounds that are engineering marvels. Together, these resilient communities of thousands solve complex problems such as determining the shortest route to a food source when many routes are viable.

Or consider seed-harvester ants. With a similar intelligence level, they must transport sufficient quantities of food at specific speeds to remain alive. To accomplish this task, they transfer food like a bucket brigade putting out a fire, but the transfer points are not fixed: an ant will carry food down the chain until it reaches the next ant. After transferring the food, it will turn back until it meets the previous ant in the chain to receive its next load. The only fixed points are the start and finish line. This flexible process is a model example of a self-sustaining system.

Now, let's consider bees. When a colony of bees grows beyond a useful size, the nest splits into two to preserve its existence. Researchers do not fully understand what variables drive this action, but nest division is a consistent pattern that has been noted around the globe.[1]

Obviously, wise, proverb-writing Solomon also noticed these little examples of the Creator's genius—species that exhibit a remarkable ability to survive and even thrive (Prov. 6:6–8). These tiny critters are perfect examples of how to sustain vital communities. Plus, they have been around for thousands of years, and based on my own warfare with them, it does not appear that they are going to disappear any time soon.

So what's the point? These seemingly simple creatures have well-defined and established practices, which are why they are still around. The scientific evidence indicates that these community-sustaining habits– or what I am calling support disciplines–are embedded parts of their culture and are passed on from one generation to the next. Let's proceed from the little creatures to us: the big creatures who are created in the image of God. Congregations that stay Christ-centered from generation to generation establish and maintain clear, support-focused disciplines that undergird their collective discipleship process. When present and consistently applied, these disciplines accelerate the exchange process of dying to self and living for Christ. Unfortunately, in too many churches– and denominations as well–these institutional-preserving disciplines become destructive forces that rule the church rather than resource the mission. The three support disciplines outlined in this chapter I call *empowering systems, aligned facilities,* and *generous stewardship.* They are the support-related practices that provide well-coordinated ministries, responsive facilities, and needed financial resources. The intended purpose of these disciplines is to sustain congregations as they move toward Christ-centeredness and the accomplishment of Christ's mission– "making disciples of all nations" (Mt. 28). This only occurs, however, when these disciplines are properly aligned to a cornerstone that recognizes and affirms Christ as King.

Sorry to be a broken record, but once again the power of and the need for a clear, Christ-centered cornerstone is obvious. When such a cornerstone is in place, these institutional-preserving disciplines are more likely to function in a supportive role, serving to help the community fulfill its discerned, God-honoring vision. In the absence of a cornerstone, though, all of these management-related disciplines easily evolve into taskmasters that seek to fill the void of visional leadership and control everything within their reach.

If you doubt me, find a church *without* a vibrant, Christ-honoring culture. Then proceed to interview various members of the community and explore with them this simple question: "*What person or group exerts the most influence on the day-to-day ministry of the church?*" Most likely, you will discover more than a few churches where the Finance Committee rules the roost. If not, the Trustees or the Personnel Committee will be the dominant force. Certainly in more than a few settings, the senior pastor will have assumed this place of authority. The Bible provides only two valid answers to this question, namely Christ (as the person: see Col. 1:18) or the Trinity (as the group). If neither is in charge, a management-related team typically steps up to the plate. In many churches, a struggle for power among several groups exists—a surefire recipe for contentiousness. That's precisely why these ministry support issues need to be approached from a perspective of disciplines meant to exalt Christ as King rather than that of a means to preserve an institution.

The Heart of the Support Disciplines

These three disciplines, though different in focus, ideally share a common set of attitudes and attributes. Before we look at the distinctive role of each discipline in depth, let's explore how they are alike when properly aligned to a Christ-centered cornerstone.

First, each of these support disciplines ideally *possesses a clear identity.* Like the larger church, teams that serve in the management of resources should have their own "DNA"—operational priorities and principles that are clearly stated, affirmed, and understood by all who participate. Predictably, any support team's identity should be closely linked to the church's mission, vision, values, and beliefs, and should define the contribution of the team and its members. Additionally, these team definitions are most effective when they are principle- and value-driven, rather than being efforts to answer every possible issue that might arise. They also benefit from frequent reassessment. One of my roles at Covenant Church is to work with the personnel team. In recent months, we have revisited our team guidelines and made some modifications to reflect the growing complexity of the church's staff. Team definitions are always a work in progress. (See appendix 4.)

Second, each of these support disciplines ideally *exists to serve others.* Some of you may consider this point repetitive and an assumed reality if the team's identity is aligned to the church's cornerstone. Frankly, I don't think it can be stated too often: *these governance-related teams only exist to serve the common good of the church community and its shared vision.* When a team possesses this kind of servant's heart, its actions will consistently assist the whole body in achieving its full kingdom potential. To this end, each time team members gather to accomplish their stated purpose, they should begin their time with prayer—and I don't mean a perfunctory thirty–second petition. I mean an intentional, spirit-altering time with God that recalibrates the participating hearts, a must-do for lay leaders—many of whom have spent their day working in a self-serving kingdom-of-the-world culture. Church staff teams are also tempted to be self-absorbed and often need to make the same shift. To that end, I have recently invited one of our church's prayer warriors to observe a key staff team that is overseeing a facility expansion process. His spirit of humility helps us stay service-focused. He is able to provide key insights to a team of intercessors who are supporting this critical phase of our church's growth.

Third, each of these support disciplines ideally *lives within its boundaries.* Collectively, their role is never to control or rule the church, but to help those on the frontlines of ministry continually answer a straightforward question: *Within the scope of our responsibilities and authority, how can we help the church move closer to fulfilling its vision?* A great example of this mentality is our Finance Team at Covenant Church. When ministry initiatives arrive on its doorstep for consideration, this group of servants is very careful to limit its assessment to the financial viability of the proposal. Needless to say, this is easier said than done. Experience, spiritual gifting, and personality naturally foster individual opinions and perspectives that may not embrace the ministry plans being considered, but that is not the question. The question the team is seeking to answer is this: does the church possess the economic capacity—both at present and in the future, if need be—to embrace the proposed initiative?

Fourth, each of the support disciplines ideally *prioritizes servant development.* Servant development is absolutely vital and is at the heart of each support discipline. Christ clearly identified making disciple-makers as the primary mission of the church. Developing disciples and overseeing their growth as kingdom servants is always more important than maintaining any institutional-preserving agenda. As already stated, we are to grow people through ministry, not grow ministry through people. Management-focused teams that deal with a wide range of topics and issues are most effective when they consistently maintain a prioritized focus on helping disciplers. (See chapter 8's discussion of the team ministry system, or C.O.S.T.) Unfortunately, management teams often have difficulty keeping disciple-making priorities front and center. My sense is that these teams often attract participants who prefer to make decisions based on efficiency and economic analysis rather than people-centered values. Christ's mission prioritizes people development, and so the support functions must as well—no ifs, ands, or buts.

The Discipline of Empowering Systems

The first of the support disciplines—*empowering systems*—is the most complex of the support disciplines. Why? Because this discipline includes a multiplicity of teams that focus on diverse agendas:

1. The financial systems that allocate resources to ministries
2. The coordination systems that integrate and oversee ministries

3. The personnel systems that ensure effective staff development and compensation
4. The pastoral systems that encourage people through personal and family crisis
5. The communication systems that provide servants with access to needed information
6. The team ministry systems (C.O.S.T.) that sustain servants who are living in community as they are being equipped for ministry
7. The spiritual leadership systems that unify the whole

Man, I'm Tired Just Thinking about It!

All of these empowering systems support the ministry disciplines detailed in the prior chapter. By definition, they work behind the scenes to help pave the way for the frontline servants. Though the teams are many, I am not suggesting that they necessarily comprise scores of lay leaders and chew up hundreds of servant hours. In fact, I would suggest the exact opposite. In a *hire...watch...pay* church, the staff is on the front line of ministry doing the work of the ministry while, by default, the laity is left as the primary overseers or what I will call administrators. As I hope I have established by now, this prototypical arrangement is neither effective nor biblical. Instead, I have suggested that staff ideally focuses its attention on training and empowering the laity for the work of ministry, which necessarily requires the paid staff to spend more time administrating the needs of the church to free up the laity. Do you see the transition? The *ministers* in the *hire...watch...pay* paradigm (staff) necessarily become the *administers* in the *invite...grow...send* model. Simultaneously, the *administers* in the *hire...watch...pay* paradigm (laity) necessarily become the *ministers* in the *invite...grow...send* model. For churches that are making this shift, staff and laity are making a 180–degree shift in focus—a wilderness experience, to be sure, after each church decides to leave Egypt and work its way to the promised land!

Obviously, laity need to have some involvement in these empowering system teams, but the goal is to streamline them as much as possible. The ultimate goal of the church is to mobilize as many folks as possible into ministry to maximize its missional impact on the community and world. Unfortunately, most churches are steeped in a complex governance structure that requires an inordinately high number of unpaid people and people hours. Based on their structure, some churches seem to operate as though the objective is to keep people busy doing administrative chores rather than free them up to do ministry. Simply put, most churches need to overhaul their empowering systems so that those systems empower people to do ministry.

The Key Principles of Empowering Systems

As a core leadership team meets together to design an empowering systems strategy that promotes congregational discipleship, it needs to bear in mind these principles:

- *Honor the Church's Cornerstone:* Obviously, the oversight systems must be in sync with one another. Predictably, this unity flows out of alignment to a common reference point—a Christ-centered cornerstone.
- *Customize Systems to Fit the Church's Unique History and Setting:* Remember the second dimension of discipleship—relevance? Each congregation needs to assess its own situation and design its empowering systems accordingly. Other congregations can serve as models, especially ones that are slightly larger, but one size does not fit all. Your setting, history, and denominational roots will help you in determining the optimal strategy that will balance staff accountability while maximizing the number of disciplers on the frontlines.
- *Be Prepared to Make New Transitions:* All churches are living and breathing organisms that necessarily need to adapt to changing times, participants, and visions. Once again, the cornerstone is the common reference point, but no approach to a ministry oversight system should be construed as permanent. Our congregation has recently empowered a *Governance Study Team* charged with designing a better way to link the efforts of all the empowering teams. One day, we will implement a new system, and it will serve us well—at least for a while. In time, it will be necessary to make another transition. That's life!
- *Clearly Define Team Purpose and Strategy of All Teams:* Who is in charge of what, and how do all the teams work in sync? Unless these questions are clearly answered, disunity and unhealthy chaos tend to reign. This is true not only for current participants, but also for those who will serve in the future. Each team also needs an orientation and training strategy that enables emerging leaders to be welcomed, trained, and relationally connected to the team (the second dimension of C.O.S.T. detailed in chapter 8). Deliberately making outsiders feel like insiders is key to sustaining servants on support teams.
- *Be Sure to Emphasize the Support Role of Empowering Teams:* I have heard it said that there are three types of people in the world: thinker-uppers, worker-outers, and getter-doners. Some folks naturally focus on the big picture and vision (thinker-uppers), while others are wired to build the related operational systems (worker-outers). The rest serve on the frontline (getter-doners). Everyone in a church needs to understand this same clarity of team roles. In our setting, we are

birthing a *Vision Alignment Team* that will partner with key staff leaders to focus on protecting the unity, purity, and long-term focus of the church—the thinking-up role. The five-to-seven members of this team are essentially the "elders" referenced by Paul in his pastoral letters (1 & 2 Timothy, Titus). The staff,[2] led by an executive team of four to six members, is primarily in charge of growing disciples in ministry, integrating related ministries, and maintaining empowered systems to accomplish the shared vision—a worker-outer role. Then, as many laity as possible are deployed into numerous frontline teams that work in sync to focus on our Great Commission mission—the getter-doner function. Here is the point: the more everyone understands these roles and has a clear picture of his or her contribution, the more effective the ministry tends to be.

- *Establish a Point Person or Team for Implementation:* I still remember playing touch football in my neighborhood as a kid and the fights we used to have in the huddle because of several pint-sized quarterback wannabes vying for control. When we would finally empower one kid to call the plays, the "worker-outer," then we could quit fighting and work together as a team. Churches also need a person or team to serve this "quarterback" role. In most churches, this person will be the pastor. In more and more churches, however, quarterbacking is the role of the executive director/pastor—a person who frees up the lead pastor to focus on preaching, teaching, spiritual leadership, and building the leadership community.[3] In the past, this staff role would only exist in larger churches with 1,000+ worshiping on weekends, but I am seeing it more and more in smaller congregations. I currently work as an executive director (since I am not ordained within this denomination) and partner with the lead pastor who is not gifted to manage the implementation systems. We describe our partnership as "Lewis and Clark" as we team together to guide our congregation on a great kingdom adventure! Though this arrangement has worked well for 3+ years, we are beginning to shift toward an "executive team" approach that will spread this quarterback role into the hands of four to six staff members. Bottom line: someone or some team needs to be empowered to execute the plays and provide a consistent direction to all the paid and unpaid players on the field. (As already stated, my bias is for staff to primarily serve in this administrative role to free up laity for the work of the ministry as described in Eph. 4:11–12.)

- *Communicate…Communicate…Communicate:* As I write, many trees in my town are making a huge mess! Spring has fully sprung, and the pollen is everywhere. Each plant seems to be trying to get the word out—"I am alive and thriving." Churches would do well to model their communication systems after nature's spring explosion—developing the kind of redundant communication systems that allow the left and right hand to stay in touch. This is one of the greatest challenges I currently face along with my staff team. Our church folks are drowning in information—e-mails, direct mail, cell phones, and the Internet all vie for their attention. As previously mentioned, we target our lay leadership with *Ministry Briefings* that provide our "ambassadors" with key information as we seek to make outsiders into insiders. But we are also finding that absolutely nothing replaces personal interaction. Together, our equipping staff will often make ten to twelve calls each to effectively reach our leadership community folks with important news.

- *Expect Healthy Chaos:* Two things are constantly shifting: the organizational needs of the church and the personal needs of ministry servants. If this assumption of mine is true, church leaders should expect a certain level of chaos. In fact, the objective of church leadership should not be a world in which everything is micro-managed, controlled, and clean; just the opposite is true. Ideally, all of the empowering teams would be in perpetual motion, adapting themselves to one another, the needs of their participants, and the church's surrounding community. As an executive director, I have to keep reminding myself of this reality because empowerment of teams within defined boundaries can be—and usually—is messy! Bottom line: the Holy Spirit is smart enough to manage the chaos as long as we stay within the biblical boundaries as defined by the church's cornerstone.

Empowering Systems Synergy—The Litmus Test for Buy In

Jesus wisely knew to how to gauge the spiritual health of an individual. He inspected the "fruit" and could draw conclusions about the whole tree by the evidence he observed on the branches, so to speak. His model is also extremely effective when working with groups. Quite frankly, the empowering systems of the church are forms of organizational fruit and reveal much about the church's spiritual vitality and direction. You just have to listen and watch—the major tasks of fruit inspectors. As a congregational coach, when I am asked to help a church get back on track, my primary focus begins with observing its history, behavior, and language. Inevitably, its stripes are revealed. Of course, I also ask questions to empowering system team leaders, but their fruit speaks for itself. My goal? To begin to understand the culture of the church and the degree to which Christ is King.

As noted already, numerous churches have taken the time to articulate portions of their DNA and tack it on their walls and Web sites. The problem lies not in the quality of their cornerstone terminology, but the breadth of their "buy in." Crafting solid and biblical DNA statements requires only a modest investment of time for a small, seasoned team of disciples. Getting the people of passion and position as well as the congregants-at-large to understand, embrace, and live into them takes a lifetime. How do I know this? Just look at Nehemiah (Neh. 4:10ff). Nehemiah presided over the return of the Jews after the Babylonian Exile and oversaw the rebuilding of Jerusalem's city wall. He successfully cast a vision and organized a whole network of servant-minded teams. Having been deployed into action, they began to make real and measurable progress—they were on their way. Within a month's time, they were scratching their heads, having forgotten their God-honoring vision. Though they started as "cathedral builders" with a clear understanding of the big picture, they quickly morphed into "stone cutters" and lost track of their direction and goals.

Such is the nature of congregational discipleship—that ongoing, relative, purposeful, contentious, and cooperative process. You just cannot stop preaching and teaching the DNA. The leadership community has to hear it all the time and at every turn. You have to vision cast constantly because some people forget and others are new to your church and have never heard it. A constant DNA reminder is vital for even those who have been thoroughly inoculated! A few pages ago, I was bragging on the members of our finance team. I noted that by design they limit their focus to strictly assessing the financial implications of a decision rather than become a directive strategy team that withholds the purse strings because they disagree with an initiative. By and large, this team has lived into this empowering DNA very well and been a great support to the church's ministry. Then, several days ago, I ended up at a finance meeting—something I rarely do in my role, and what do you know?—one person started to get on his soap box about a proposed initiative that he disagreed with. What a "Nehemiah" experience! We were on a roll, everything was going smoothly, and boom!—a support team jumps the railroad tracks and starts to act like a thinker-upper team. Ultimately, it turned out okay. The team leader gently pulled in the reins and reminded folks of the team's affirmed DNA—a focus on financial viability. Think Nehemiah, and assume people are quick to forget the church's God-honoring cornerstone!

A Quick Summary

Remember the Scriptural mandate that "the last shall be first, and the first shall be last"? This order upside-downs what we would expect to work. At first glance, perhaps you are thinking that these management-related teams are a little too upside-down because they seem to support rather than control. Think of it this way: this approach is a practical and biblical way of liberating all of us—staff and laity alike—to accomplish the work that Jesus Christ would have us do. When properly exercised, the discipline of *empowering systems* is a powerful means to encourage a church to exchange obsolete management strategies that promote control for streamlined ministry systems that help a church maximize its missional purpose. Well-crafted management guidelines for church life provide freedom for the Spirit's winds to blow in and through the church's people to accomplish great things for God.

The Discipline of Aligned Facilities

Whereas empowering systems facilitates Christ's mission by providing the management infrastructure, the second support discipline—*aligned facilities*—leverages the church's physical resources for the same God-honoring purposes. Since the vast majority of established churches have secured space and related equipment for their ministries, the core issue of this discipline is always alignment. For sure, a church's facilities are always aligned to something, and so the key question becomes: To w*hom or what are they aligned*? Now we are right back to the systemic question for all churches: Who is in charge? If the heart of the congregation is more focused on its own agenda, it tends to enshrine and preserve the church's facilities on behalf of club members. However, if Jesus is on the throne of the church's heart, then its people will tend to align facility usage to their faith community's unique vision and His eternal agenda—the Great Commission. The goal of this discipline, therefore, is to encourage a church to keep exchanging its own agenda for Christ's missional objectives facilities-wise. Once again, a subservient relationship between this discipline and a Christ-centered cornerstone is of paramount importance and defines both the nature and parameters of godly alignment.

Why would the alignment of church facilities to the Great Commission serve to accelerate a church's movement toward Christ-centeredness? The answer to this question is as close as your kids or anyone else's, for that matter. My sense is that my three boys are pretty typical of children all around the world. One of the very first words they learned was "mine." In no uncertain terms, their use of this powerful word clearly communicated their desire to control everything within their reach. They did not see objects within their world as gifts, but as things to be controlled with absolute rights of ownership. (This worldview was especially true of the youngest, who figured out very quickly that competition was always ready to pounce on all things within his grasp.)

Now let me ask you: as adults, are we any different? All too often, we forget that God is indeed the owner of all things, a rock-solid reality in the Scriptures (Ps. 24:1). As the Bible clearly states, all that we are and all we possess belong to the Creator. We are simply managers with no ownership privileges. The irony is that the only way to learn how to share *is* to share. The very action of sharing shapes our hearts, just as Jesus stated: "Where your treasure is, there your heart will be also" (Mt. 6:21). Notice the sequence? Our *treasures* (actions) shape our *hearts* (attitudes). When a church shares its facility freely to maximize its kingdom impact, its heart is moved closer and closer to Christ-centeredness. Undoubtedly, the discipline of aligned facilities steers a church to use its building for Christ's kingdom-growing agenda. Once again, a WWCCD mentality—What Would Christ's Church Do if our facilities were at His disposal?—is key. Would He want us to keep them off limits to outsiders? Or would He want them to be wisely used to advance His church's vision? The answers to the questions are easy to grasp, but much more difficult to put into practice.

Let me digress right in the middle of this discipline to review once again the essence of congregational spiritual disciplines. I consistently find that some people struggle to understand the role of these disciplines as "process strategies" rather than cause-and-effect, action steps that automatically result in God's blessing. Personally, I would prefer the latter—a sure-fire recipe and no-fail directions that would guarantee the anointing of God. But our God is much more creative as He searches out the depths of our loyalty and love. Congregational spiritual vitality is a matter of the heart, not the result of some predetermined action step. The disciplines detailed in this section don't make a church spiritually alive, in the same way that the personal disciplines of reading the Bible or praying don't guarantee the blessing of God's power to us individually. Spiritual vitality is a gift of God and flows out of faithful obedience (Jn. 14:15–17)—a cooperative process of transformation greatly enhanced by both personal and congregational disciplines.

The cornerstone, ministry, and support disciplines simply encourage the community of faith to turn away from its natural self-serving tendencies and embrace a kingdom lifestyle. Being a club is easy. Being a church is tough. We have to die to ourselves before we can faithfully realize our kingdom calling. Once again, that's where the disciplines come in. They are formational strategies whose ultimate target is the heart—the systemic issue for both me, and us.

The Key Principles of Aligned Facilities

As a core leadership team meets together to design an aligned facilities strategy that promotes congregational discipleship, it needs to bear in mind these relevant principles:

- *Define Alignment Clearly:* Alignment is the key issue. The leadership community will need to continually wrestle with the nature and specifics of its church's calling. The process is ongoing, especially for the "thinker-uppers" who necessarily need to keep discerning the special burden that Christ has placed on the heart of the congregation. The clearer the vision the easier facility alignment is. When addressing the need for clear priorities, author Stephen Covey often uses a terrarium to make a crucial point. He will bring a bowl on stage containing several big rocks completely surrounded by smaller rocks, sand, and water all the way to the brim. Covey then makes the point that you have to put the big rocks in first before anything else. If you put the little rocks and sand in first, the big rocks will not fit. But the little rocks *will* fit if the big ones go in first.) At Covenant, our top, visional priorities—or "big rocks"—stand out in bold relief and provide a clear path to the church's emerging direction and the use of our facilities.
- *Think Long Term:* The wise stewardship of space and equipment requires long-term thinking, especially for churches in the process of expanding their space. Whether a church is young, old, or somewhere in between, ministry leaders need to think beyond their own immediate needs. How will today's decisions help or hinder future generations in being faithful to Christ's calling? Wise leaders keep asking this question. Recently, Covenant contracted to buy thirty additional acres of land for its future ministry. We could certainly get by with less in the next decade, but deliberate, long-term thinking paves the way for our grandkids and beyond.
- *Design Flexible Space:* A natural extension of this long-term thinking principle is flexibility. I am constantly amazed at how church facilities are designed in ways that limit future usability. Expansion options, load-bearing walls, infant/toddler care, and parking are just a sampling of the issues needing long-term perspectives in the planning process. If handled thoughtfully and wisely, current leadership can empower future disciples with the opportunity to make facility adjustments with minimum interruption and maximum impact.

- *Craft Clear, Decision-making Guidelines:* Those empowered to manage facilities have tough issues to resolve as they balance all the various ministry needs, so clear guidelines are a must. Within these guidelines, segmenting the types of ministry events a church sponsors is a good idea. At Covenant, we distinguish among core, partnership, and community ministries. *Core ministries* are essential church ministries, such as weekend worship. *Partnership ministries* are those initiated by the laity that complement the DNA, but are not absolutely essential for the vision to be realized. (Our "Meals Ministry" for the sick is one example.) *Community ministries* are led by externally based organizations with whom the church is in some way linked. Accordingly, our facility guidelines reflect these three levels—a differentiation that helps us balance our priorities with the needs of our surrounding community.

- *Craft Clear Boundaries for Users:* Defined boundaries for how facilities are managed, reserved, and used are a must. If these boundaries are not in place, communicated, and understood, the congregation will perceive that the facility is tightly guarded and controlled; and, believe me, contention is right around the corner.

- *Be Careful with Endowments:* Keeping facilities in good working order takes money, especially as the years pass. Some churches, in concert with well-meaning and generous servants, have endowed the ongoing care of the facilities. The benefits of having these resources are self-evident, but a downside does exist. Does the endowment prevent future changes in the facility? Does the endowment in any way make the facility a shrine that has to be protected from outsiders? Has the endowment been written so that the facility can be remodeled with the natural development of the church's growth and needs? Does the endowment strongly reinforce Christ's proper place on the throne of the church's heart, or does it put certain individuals or groups in charge? All of these questions must be dealt with carefully so that the endowment is effective and honoring to God as well as to the church's vision.

- *Beware of Naming Rights as Well:* Churches that are expanding their space sometimes use "naming rights" as an enticement to help fund the project. I have two concerns about this practice. *First,* naming rights communicate a spiritual message regarding power in the congregation, the purpose for the facility, and a preoccupation with recognition. This strategy generally reinforces a club mentality and works against the notion of congregational discipleship—a deliberate movement toward Christ-centeredness. *Second,* naming rights tend to hamper future leaders from making necessary changes. When this occurs, the priority of ministry takes a backseat to the preservation of the past. The result: alignment to the church's discerned vision is severely compromised. Always protect Christ's place as the Head of the church no matter what the cost!

- *Avoid Naming Space after Groups or Congregants:* Along the same lines as above, I strongly urge your church to avoid memorializing church space by naming it after any one person or group, because this strategy often becomes a barrier down the road. A church I recently consulted for had a terrific large-group space dominated on Sunday mornings by an aging Sunday school class. Many years ago, this class of younger adults filled the room and was the source of much vitality. Today, this group is composed of a half-dozen adults who could easily move to a smaller space and make way for a larger class, but the name on the door keeps them right where they are. Instead, consider naming space after biblical characters, thus conveying the spirit of Christ-centered ministry, outreach, and the Great Commission.

- *Organize a Steering Team When Expanding:* The adage "well begun is half done" applies big time when a church considers expansion. A good start on this venture means putting in place an oversight team that will help assure well-designed buildings, good stewardship of church resources, broad congregational ownership, and a timely integration with ongoing ministries. It will also enable the church to avoid a spirit of disunity and concentrate on living into its vision and mission. As the church begins to think about expanding, it needs to be careful about what the oversight team is called. For instance, I generally encourage churches to utilize a name like "Steering Team" to emphasize the need for this group to focus on the entire scope of the project. Ideally, a steering team provides both long-term vision and practical leadership as it empowers a number of subteams that are attentive to various "tracks." These tracks flesh out the various levels of the project and address the following types of elements:

1. The obvious brick-and-mortar planning track—*how the project is designed*
2. The heart transformation track—*how the project relates to the church's walk of faith*
3. The core ideology track—*how the project relates to the church's vision and mission*
4. The financial track—*how the project relates to the church's economics*
5. The staff track—*how the project relates to the focus of current and future staff*

6. The ministry systems track—*how the project relates to existing congregational systems*
7. The new ministries track—*how the project relates to opportunities for new ministry*

The responsibility of the *steering team,* therefore, is to define, launch, and coordinate the teams needed to complete the facility expansion process in keeping with the tracks outlined above.

- *Birth a Team of Levites:* The Old Testament role of the Levites sets a powerful precedent for congregational leaders as they seek to sustain the faith community's space. The Levites' responsibilities extended well beyond a priestly function to include the oversight of the temple after it was built. Who are those individuals within your congregation who have a passion for this upkeep ministry? In my experience, this team often serves as a good front door to get men who are comfortable working with their hands connected to the church's mission.
- *Don't Forget to Align the Budget:* Paying for utilities and generally maintaining a current facility are usually understood by all as fixed costs—ones that are nonnegotiable and annually built into the budget. But churches often forget to include the costs of the "big rocks," especially when planning for improvements. Churches benefit from answering these questions: *What are the costs associated with the emerging priorities of the church? What new space will be needed? Will new furnishings, computers, and related equipment need to be purchased?* Let me make several suggestions. *First,* for smaller initiatives, establish a separate, yearly *capital improvements budget* that parallels the church's annual operating budget and includes special one-time expenditures for the next year. (The source of these monies is typically either the anticipated pledges or undesignated reserves.) This strategy prevents these stand-alone items from becoming embedded in the operating budget as permanent costs. *Second,* when facing large projects linked to a capital campaign, dedicate a portion of funds to soft costs such as staffing, furnishings, or mission work. In a former congregation, we used 20 percent of money raised in a campaign to hire multiple part-time staff for the newly expanded facility as well as help build a new hospital in Haiti. I typically find that a church's business people grasp this integrated approach quickly. (In industry, money borrowed for expansion is never solely dedicated to brick and mortar. Inevitably, it capitalizes a number of expenses including new employees, start-up costs including equipment, as well as inventory.) Capitalize the whole ministry project—not just the space!

The Sure Sign of Success–Velveteen Rabbit Facilities

When I was a young tyke, I loved Freddy Frog. In fact, I loved Freddy to death. Freddy was a stuffed animal I carried everywhere. I don't mean just some places. For a time, Freddy was like a conjoined twin–where I went, he went. Obviously, over time Freddy took a beating. Arms and legs had to be reattached, and, thankfully, my mother was an able seamstress! As much as a toddler could love something, I loved Freddy. Freddy was my "Velveteen Rabbit"–loved but a little worn around the edges. Like Freddy, the Velveteen Rabbit transitioned from a pristine, new toy to a treasured friend, and, in the process, showed all the signs of that love. Likewise, church space should take on the same mantle. This is, I believe, the sure sign of good stewardship–a facility that begins as a new building but is transformed into an alive and greatly loved friend as it gets used for kingdom building day after day.

Jesus is not interested in shrines, but in useful space and resources that are leveraged for the benefit of His mission. As we use new facilities, they become tangible tools that help people grow in their faith with the clear expectation that the brick and mortar incurs bumps and bruises along the way. Build a facility to facilitate growth, and watch in amazement as the Lord honors both!

Quick Summary

Youngsters quickly and predictably learn the word "mine." However, disciples and communities of faith need to "put away childish things" (1 Cor. 13:11) and learn the word "God's." That's what church facilities are–God's! When properly exercised, the discipline of *aligned facilities* is a powerful means to encourage church members to exchange a worldly mindset that church property is theirs for a biblical mindset that God is the rightful owner of all things. Once again, when faithful followers let God be God, the wind of the Spirit is at their backs and not in their faces.

The Discipline of Generous Stewardship

The discipline of empowering systems undergirds Christ's mission by providing an essential management infrastructure. The discipline of aligned facilities leverages the church's physical resources for the same God-honoring purposes. The third support discipline–*generous steward-ship*–links the faithful tithing of Christ's followers with the economic needs of His Body–the Church. Unfortunately, in most churches, stewardship ministry is associated with fund raising and has a strong negative connotation. Such a view misses the heart of the Bible's teaching on generosity. The challenge, therefore, is to transition this ministry from an institutional agenda that focuses on fund raising to one that prioritizes heart raising.

When I was in my mid-thirties, I was hired as a jack-of-all-trades for a church of a thousand in North Carolina. My business background and training allowed me to fill several business-related roles, while my theological training and experience paved the way for my focus on the church's teaching, small group, and lay mobilization ministries. Though I wore many hats, the position fit me well—except for the one dreaded assignment, namely "stewardship." Frankly, I am a wimp when it comes to "hitting people up" for cash; I'm just not gifted at closing that kind of "sale." During my first year on the job, I learned some biblical principles that completely changed my attitude and understanding. By the time I left the staff of that church eight years later, stewardship was one of my favorite ministry roles.

I learned a key lesson: stewardship ministry is actually a discipleship ministry that emphasizes the teaching of God's Word. Accordingly, I discovered that this ministry is not about the need of the institution to get money, but about the need of the giver to give generously. Once I understood these key concepts, I no longer had to develop strategies to ask people to financially support the church's agenda. All I had to do was teach disciples the biblical standard of generosity and challenge them to be faithful to Christ's calling on their lives. This changed my whole outlook on the ministry. Instead of dreading it, I actually looked forward to it because I love to teach God's Word. When disciples understand and obey God's economic principles, the collective economic needs of the church are naturally, and even joyfully, met.

Over the years, I have also learned how powerful generosity is at shaping the hearts of disciples, both individually and collectively. Jesus obviously understood the reality that our hearts follow our actions: "Where your treasure is, there your heart will be also" (Mt. 6:21). The power of generosity to shape us corporately is the essence of this congregational discipline. When we pool our sacrificial tithes for kingdom causes, it accelerates the transformation of our church's heart—moving us from a mindset of hoarding what we think is ours to a mindset of yielding all of our lives to Him (Josh. 24:23).

The Key Principles of Generous Stewardship

As a core leadership team meets together to design a generous stewardship strategy that promotes congregational discipleship, it needs to bear in mind these relevant principles:

- *Adopt New Language to Help Refocus:* The word *stewardship* tends to have a negative connotation and is often associated with fund raising. Leaders must find new terms and phrases that help convey the heart of the ministry. "Generous" is much more descriptive of God's actions and desire for our lives and so is included in Covenant's stewardship ministry's slogan: *Unleashing the Power of Generosity.* We have played off of Willow Creek's "Good Sense" phraseology and call our ministry the "Good Cents Ministry." Whatever works to communicate biblical themes in your context is the right one for your church.

- *Assume Folks Have Never Been Taught Biblical Standards for Managing Their Finances:* The sooner you embrace this assumption, along with the two that follow, the sooner you will be able to accelerate generous stewardship in your church. The vast majority of us, even as church-goers, have never heard sound biblical teaching in the area of finances and possessions. Instead, we have heard the steady drumbeat of consumerism since we were toddlers. Companies don't purchase commercial time on TV because they want to make us better people, but because they want us to buy their stuff. Our natural tendency to be self-serving, combined with a lifelong exposure to media messages defining our worth by the things we acquire, is great for advertising but toxic to our hearts. The antidote? Solid teaching from God's Word that directly lays out the principles and boundaries regarding God's plan for us to use things wisely and His desire for us to experience the power and joy of generosity.

- *Assume Folks Have Forgotten the God-honoring Vision of the Church:* Another thing you can count on is that your community of faith will forget its unique vision just as quickly as Nehemiah's craftsmen forgot their wall-restoration objective. Not only do disciples need to know biblical generosity, they also need to understand how their giving resources the church's vision. Help them make this important connection by providing clear, consistent messages.

- *Assume Folks Distrust the Church's Leadership:* Trust, especially with handling others' money, is something that needs to be earned over and over again. Diligent accountability is the one thing leadership can provide that will dispel any hint of financial mismanagement. Conduct annual audits, and publish them. Do not allow any secret accounts to exist. Be forthcoming to a fault. If any action smells fishy, don't do it!

- *Reclassify the Stewardship Ministry Under Adult Discipleship:* Generosity is not about the business side of the church's ministry, but the heart side. Accordingly, like all the other spiritual disciplines, categorize and link this ministry with the other adult spiritual formation ministries.

- *Teach and Communicate This Theme Year-round:* Dedicate three to four consecutive weeks a year to a special focus on generosity. Preaching and teaching the "full counsel of God" dictates that generosity be frankly talked about, just as Jesus talked about it. Stewardship themes should be highlighted year-round through testimonials or preaching points. Stories of generous disciples and the benefits of faithful obedience are both uplifting and convicting as your church embraces the discipline of generous stewardship.

- *Only Unveil the Budget Afterward:* Don't publish the church's budgetary needs prior to the three to four–week teaching emphasis on generosity. How much disciples should contribute to the ministries of the church has nothing to do with the church's budget. The Bible teaches proportional giving of our "first fruits" to God's "storehouse," not reaching some preestablished, corporate goal. Teach disciples to be faithful financially, and then let the finance team craft a related budget after commitments are made. Remember: stewardship is not about the need of the institution to receive, but about the need of the giver to give. Showing the budget up front before encouraging people's hearts to be generous reinforces the former and erodes the latter!

- *Provide Multiple Entry Points for Learning:* Fostering generous disciples within your church setting requires a multilevel teaching ministry. Think of this ministry as a cafeteria, and provide choices: from easy-to-swallow gelatin desserts to more meaty entrees. Fortunately, you can select from an increasing number of effective curriculum choices. For many churches like ours, Crown Ministry provides a variety of resources and is a great starting point. Crown's materials have helped thousands of churches establish a basic strategy that balances formational Bible studies and personal accountability.[4]

- *Link Generosity to Results:* After the budget is formed and as the ministry year unfolds, be sure that people know how their generosity is resulting in changed lives. One of the easiest ways to do this is with a "statement stuffer" that accompanies a participant's giving update. In crafting these communiqués, also be sure to directly reinforce the church's vision as well as underscore the current "big rocks."

- *Communicate Faithfulness, Not Dues:* One of my pet peeves is how much church giving statements look like bills to be paid, as though they were club dues. My suggestion? Get rid of see-through envelopes, redesign the layout, adopt grace-filled color, and make the statements look more like birth announcements! We are to be joyful givers, not bill payers!

- *Use Little Opportunities to Grow Big Hearts:* Some folks believe that designated giving erodes support for the basic operating needs of the church. (By designated giving, I mean stand-alone gifts for special needs. A recent example in 2005 was the Indonesian tsunami relief effort and the Gulf Coast hurricane rebuilding.) Certainly, if a church constantly lifted up special needs, I am sure such designated requests for money would undermine the bread-and-butter "first fruits" giving. But I would suggest to you that seasonal and periodic opportunities to fund special needs actually foster generous hearts, especially for spiritual youngsters. Here is how it works. Folks who have never tasted the joy of giving hear about an opportunity. The Spirit breaks through to their hearts, and they open their checkbooks to help meet a specific need. Suddenly, they learn a new lesson: generosity brings great joy. Jesus knew this truth when he linked our treasures to our hearts. Helping young disciples experience this spiritual truth can result in big changes!

Unleashing the Power

As a congregational coach and teacher, I sometimes like to drop verbal bombs—hyperboles that overstate the case, but make an important point. This technique seems to keep listeners mentally engaged as I communicate kingdom themes. For example, sometimes while teaching on the power of spiritual disciplines to change our hearts, I will say something outrageous, such as, "I hate to pray!" I'll make this dire pronouncement several times with gusto and then ask the audience why they think I hate to pray so much. I usually get several erroneous responses, before I share that I hate to die to self. I hate to admit that I am not in control. I hate to acknowledge my need, and so forth. As I have been emphasizing all along, embracing God's agenda always begins with letting go of our own. Transformation through prayer is painful—which is why I also hate to read God's Word, worship, fast, serve, and give!

So what's the point? Expect the people of your church to detest all of the congregational spiritual disciplines I have been describing in this section. Expect them to hate the cornerstone disciplines as Christ is secured in His rightful place on the throne. Expect them to despise the ministry disciplines as Jesus' equipping methodologies are put into practice. Expect them to abhor the support disciplines—especially this last one—as each undergirds the church's disciple-making efforts. These nine disciplines for Christ's church are hurtful strategies that erode self-worship and painfully propel the community of faith toward Christ-centeredness. Indeed, this transformational process demands a radical change of culture, but therein lies its power.

The vision of our church's "Good Cents Ministry" is to "*unleash the power of generosity in Pitt County and around the world through the teaching of God's Word.*" We are convinced that as we collectively align our financial lives to God's biblical prescription, we will witness the power of pooled resources to make a kingdom impact as well as the power for disciples to be set free from the bondage of materialism. Over five years ago, our church saw firsthand generosity's power to kill self-interest and embrace God's kingdom focus. Our gifts flowed unselfishly to nearby communities devastated by the floodwaters of Hurricane Floyd. That communal experience fundamentally changed our church from the inside out. More recently, the Indonesian tsunami and two Gulf Coast hurricanes gave us a humbling opportunity to exercise the discipline of generous stewardship and experience a strong gust of Holy Spirit's wind as we sacrificially shared.

So, what's next for us? An upcoming facility expansion project will surely have the same impact our last expansion did. At first, we will come kicking and screaming to the altar of our self-interest. There, we will painfully ponder changes in our financial lives, prioritize Christ's vision, make sacrificial commitments—and then, blessedly, we will experience the renewal of our hearts. Why? That's just the way it is; authentic spiritual power is always unleashed by radical, faithful obedience.

A Quick Summary

Jesus constantly addressed our relationship with the material world. The word *give* is one of the most common words in the Bible, whether the context is our need to give or God's example of grace-filled giving to us (Jn. 3:16). When we model our lives after His example, we become the benefactors, for it is "more blessed to give than to receive" (Acts 20:35). When properly exercised, *generous stewardship* is a powerful means to encourage a church to exchange the obligation of paying "club dues" for the joy of sharing God's blessings to make disciples of all nations. Congregational generosity is a common indicator of the presence of God's Spirit and is a visible witness to a world yearning for meaning and significance.

Emerging Truths about Congregational Spiritual Disciplines

Cornerstone, ministry, and *support disciplines:* nine process strategies that transform a church's heart and its culture. They are formational exercises that accelerate God's people toward Christ-centeredness—an ongoing process of exchanging our human agendas for God's that results in the anointing by God's Spirit (Jn. 14:15–17).[5]

As I conclude, let me highlight who typically empowers each of these three categories of disciplines. I recommend that the church's executive leadership—some combination of staff and lay elders—focus on the cornerstone disciplines of cornerstone discernment, leadership alignment, and vision casting. However your church defines these spiritual overseers, this group is primarily responsible for maintaining the congregation's unity, purity, and ongoing movement toward Christ's unique calling as defined by a shared cornerstone.

Ideally, the ministry disciplines of relevant worship, spiritual formation, and lay mobilization are then acted on by the church's equippers (Eph. 4:11). These disciples focus their time and energy on training, coordinating, and empowering ministry servants (Eph. 4:12). Paid ministry leaders serve as the primary equippers and "air traffic controllers" to implement Jesus' disciple-making methods within the context of the church's God-honoring vision. However, make no mistake—numerous unpaid leaders should also make vital contributions as equipping leaders, a sure sign of invite…grow…send.

Finally, the support disciplines of empowering systems, aligned facilities, and generous stewardship are best realized through the combined efforts of both staff and lay administrators. The majority of these teams are connected to one another through the established governance structure of the church and necessarily adopt the common heart attributes and attitudes detailed at the beginning of this chapter.

As we review what we have learned, a handful of principles will strengthen our understanding and capacity to provide effective leadership:

- *Resourcing Christ's mission and people begins with a supportive management infrastructure—the discipline of empowering systems.* The focus of these organizational teams is not to preserve institutional control, but to help servants on the front lines of ministry. Through setting clear boundaries and exhibiting humility, they maximize the kingdom impact of the church within its sphere of influence.
- *Christ's disciple-making mandate benefits from facilities that are flexible, coordinated, and available for kingdom purposes—the discipline of aligned facilities.* The congregation's tangible assets are tools to reach both inside and beyond the walls of the church. Ideally, they are designed and built wisely, cared for constantly, and used for mission incessantly.
- *The Great Commission is effectively funded by emphasizing the need of the giver to give, not the need of the institution to receive—the discipline of generous*

stewardship. As we faithfully return the first fruits of our labor to Christ's storehouse, the power of God's Spirit is unleashed within our personal and collective lives. Individually, we experience freedom from the consumptive values of this world. Collectively, we witness, rejoice in, and are transformed by the kingdom impact of our pooled resources. Indeed, sharing is far better than hoarding. And watch out! To borrow a title from one of C. S. Lewis's books, once you learn generosity, you will be *surprised by joy!*

My final thought is borrowed from Joshua and are his last words to the people of Israel—they say it all: "[T]hrow away the foreign gods that are among you and yield your hearts to the LORD" (Josh. 24:23).

Epilogue

"You have persevered and have endured hardships for my name,
and have not grown weary. Yet I hold this against you:
You have forsaken your first love.
Remember the height from which you have fallen!
Repent and do the things you did at first."

JESUS (Rev. 2:3–4a)

Remember my friend Tom and his clubby church?

Well, he is no longer serving that congregation. His efforts to reshape the church's culture resulted in his being asked to leave. Though he tried his best, Tom sadly discovered that the community was unwilling to exchange its self-serving ways for a Christ-centered paradigm that prioritized disciple making. At one time, I am sure that the members' hearts yielded to Jesus, the risen Christ, and were singularly dedicated to His missional agenda. For whatever reason, they had drifted away as they became increasingly comfortable with a closed community that met their social needs. Forsaking Jesus rarely happens overnight, but the vast majority of congregations travel this same path. In so doing, they forfeit their identity as Christian churches. If I had known then what I know now, I would have given Tom some very specific counsel. Instead, let me pass it along to you.

First, understand that a church's faithfulness parallels our own discipleship journey—the process is ongoing, relative, purposeful, contentious, and cooperative. Accordingly, the transformation of the church's culture is a God thing, will not happen quickly (usually five to seven years), and can only occur if and when the church returns to its first love, Jesus Christ. The heart of the matter is the church's willingness to collectively surrender to Christ as King and Lord, square one of spiritual vitality.

Second, begin preaching and teaching both the *message* of hope and the *method* by which that hope is to be taken to the ends of the earth.

Detail what Jesus said and how He organized the early disciples. Move on to Paul and the Early Church for additional examples of Spirit-empowered communities of faith. Pray often, intensely, and earnestly. Look for those people of passion whose eyes responsively light up. If the church's heart is receptive, its pulse will quicken in response. The "soil" of your church is now ready to be plowed and planted with strategies that foster vitality—congregational spiritual disciplines.

Next, introduce the "cornerstone" disciplines as process strategies designed to help secure Christ as Head of the church. In so doing, launch a team that will guide the process of cornerstone discernment. Once this team is in place and working, begin to form a leadership community that includes both the people of passion *and* the people of position. Continually embed the church's Christ-centered cornerstone into these disciples. Assuming that the process is gaining some traction, cast a vision for this missional cornerstone for the larger congregation in a way that is compelling, visual, and consistent. Remember, however, that all these wonderful-sounding activities come with a clear warning: these formational strategies will not always result in their desired effect, for they are spiritual disciplines—a means for encouraging cooperation with God's Spirit. In more than a few contexts, pastors like Tom will discover that the church just wants a club president, not a disciple-maker.

When you find your church is ready to embrace and live out a Christ-centered cornerstone, you will then want to establish Christ's disciple-making methodology—the "ministry" disciplines for adults, students, and children. Begin with making worship relevant for both current disciples and prospective guests. In so doing, be sure that the church's welcoming ministries are aligned to this same audience. Build upon this mission-minded focus with the second ministry discipline: spiritual formation. Craft a series of appealing learning opportunities that equip participants with a solid biblical foundation. Leverage both the power of small groups and the effectiveness of large-group teaching with a cafeteria of choices. In due time, utilize the discipline of lay mobilization to create the dynamic systems that will allow emerging ambassadors to find their place in ministry and become faithful, fruitful, and fulfilled servants. As they discover the joy of being children of the King and doing ministry for His glory, they will make God famous. All who see them will want to know the "reason for the hope" they have (1 Pet. 3:15). Can you feel the winds of the Spirit picking up?

As momentum builds, supply these disciple-making ministries with essential resources—the "support" disciplines. Establish a series of empowering teams that work in sync with one another to provide a dynamic, effective infrastructure. The formation of this well-coordinated system will require ample doses of time, patience, and clarity. Do all of this with a singular goal in mind: to assist the servants on the front line of ministry. Align the church's facility and resources to the cornerstone as well. The purpose of the congregation's space and equipment is nothing more than to help sustain its outwardly focused mission. Finally, be sure to preach and teach a biblical emphasis on generosity. This final discipline—a focus on the need of givers to give—results in financial first fruits that fuel the congregation's God-honoring vision.

So, why bother with all these disciplines? Your church's devotion to Christ is a matter of the heart. And the time is now to cooperate with God's Spirit in facilitating its return to Him, the First Love, the only Love that will matter in the end.

> *"For the eyes of the LORD range throughout the earth to strengthen those whose hearts are fully committed to him."*
>
> 2 CHRONICLES 16:9a

APPENDIX 1

A Disciple-making Disciple

"Ambassador"

An ambassador is someone who represents the interests of their "native land" in and to a foreign land. They should not be seen as experts, because they aren't. They are well-rounded disciples who have discovered their special abilities and gifts bestowed by the Spirit. They combine these with the basic competencies of ministry, which they have learned through the laboratory of life. Scripture indicates that their lives are marked by a handful of qualities and skills as detailed below.

Relies on Jesus Christ: The central driving principle of an ambassador's life is a relationship with and a dependence upon Jesus as both Lord and Savior. *Lord* implies an ownership and authority to which they have submitted. *Savior* indicates recognition of sin and the resulting need for and reliance upon Jesus' work on the cross. God is actively and intimately involved in their lives. This intimacy is cultivated through a commitment to and practice of the foundational disciplines of prayer, study of scripture, fellowship, regular worship, service, and generosity. Ambassadors

1. worship weekly unless circumstances conspire to prevent this;
2. participate weekly/bi-weekly in a group that prioritizes the spiritual growth of its members;
3. comfortably and regularly pray with and for others;
4. serve in an area that reflects their passion, giftedness, and personality;
5. prioritizes the church as they grow in the grace of giving toward the biblical standard of a tithe and beyond.

Committed to Family Relationships: A single or married ambassador understands God's design for and the importance of family. Ambassadors realize that if these relationships are not in order, they will be ineffective in ministry. Those that are married understand that this covenant relationship is a model to the world of Christ's relationship to the Church. In like manner, parents embrace their responsibility to love their children and to prioritize their spiritual needs. Ambassadors

1. prioritize family time and see this as ministry;
2. address family concerns and seek help when appropriate;

3. are intentional about learning how to strengthen their family system;
4. pray for (and with as able) their family on a regular basis.

Grasps the Biblical Story: Ambassadors have a basic handle on God's Word. They understand the central message of the Bible and can communicate the plan of salvation to others. They are in process, growing in their personal understanding and application of the Word as well as imparting truth to those around them. Ambassadors

1. understand and can explain the basic structure of the Bible and its various literary forms;
2. understand and can explain the Bible's basic outline and relate it to God's plan of salvation along with key passages;
3. confidently utilize the basics of Bible interpretation and related resources to discern the intended meaning of a passage.

Affirms Own and Others Giftedness: Ambassadors understand their unique giftedness and utilize their gifts to build up the Body and minister to others as God directs them. They recognize and affirm the giftedness of others. They make themselves available to ministry. Ambassadors

1. are confident and knowledgeable of their own giftedness based on ministry experience and related study;
2. understand and can explain the distinction between spiritual gifts, roles, disciplines, and fruit.

Lives in Community: Ambassadors embrace the fact that spiritual growth always occurs within the context of community. Accordingly, they are committed to mentoring relationships, small groups, and ministry teams as an essential part of personal growth and a fundamental building block of the church (as noted in the first category). Ambassadors

1. understand and can confidently provide shepherding leadership for either a mentoring relationship or small group.

Translates the Good News: Ambassadors live out their faith in such a way that others are attracted to them. They have the skills to share with others the hope they have within them in a meaningful and relevant way. They intentionally build loving relationships with non-believers to pave the way to naturally share their faith with them. Ambassadors

1. confidently share with others their faith journey along with God's plan of salvation;
2. understand and can coach others in the basics of relational evangelism.

Relates with Open Ears and Eyes: Ambassadors continue to develop and utilize the skills of active listening, effective speaking, and discernment to serve alongside others. They are aware of the affect that both verbal and non-verbal messages communicate to others. Discernment gives them the wisdom to recognize error and dysfunction and to choose helpful strategies for ministering to others. Ambassadors

1. regularly utilize skills of reflective listening;
2. capably discern the context and setting of all interpersonal communication so as to avoid inappropriate triangulation and gamesmanship.

Committed to Covenant Church: Ambassadors understand the biblical purposes of a Christian church. They understand and are committed to fulfilling Christ's mission through Covenant. An ambassador welcomes accountability to the common boundaries of Covenant's ministry, namely its values, beliefs, vision, and mission. Ambassadors

1. understand and can explain the fundamental values, beliefs, and mission of Covenant Church;
2. are able to interpret its vision for ministry to those within and outside the walls.

APPENDIX 2

Covenant United Methodist Church Staff Values*

The body is a unit, though it is made up of many parts; and though all its parts are many, they form one body. So it is with Christ...so that there should be no division in the body, but that its parts should have equal concern for each other. If one part suffers, every part suffers with it; if one part is honored, every part rejoices with it.

1 CORINTHIANS 12:12, 25–26

The staff of Covenant United Methodist Church, in partnership with one another, has discerned these values to guide our collective journey of faith. By the grace of God, we aspire to live by these values in all that we do.

Excellence–"Whatever you do, work at it with all your heart, as working for the Lord, not for men, since you know that you will receive an inheritance from the Lord as a reward. It is the Lord Christ you are serving." Colossians 3:23–24

Using Jesus as our model, Excellence means:
- Seeking the Pleasure of God alone
- Being Christ-like in heart and mind
- Doing One's Sacrificial Best
- Finishing–hearing God say "Well Done"

Teamwork–"Two are better than one because they have good return for their work: If one falls down, his friend can help him up. But pity the man who falls and has no one to help him up! Though one may be overpowered, two can defend themselves. A cord of three strands is not quickly broken." Ecclesiastes 4:9–10, 12

Using the Trinity as our model, Teamwork means:
- Working together to fulfill the mission of the church
- Recognizing and utilizing the spiritual gifts and talents of the team

---

*This is a reprint of the statement of staff values from Covenant United Methodist Church in Winterville, North Carolina.

- Serving the team as a vital contributor
- Encouraging team members in their areas of responsibility

Trust—"Now it is required that those who have been given a trust must prove faithful." 1 Corinthians 4:2

Using a Disciple's relationship with God as our model, Trust means:

- Being dependable on a daily basis
- Being consistently reliable
- Working to develop authentic relationships through honesty and accountability
- Esteeming the importance of confidentiality and personal integrity

Respect—"And the second is like it: 'Love your neighbor as yourself.'" Matthew 22:39

Using the second greatest commandment as our model, Respect means:

- Honoring and supporting the ideas and gifts of others
- Relating to one another in humility
- Embracing the unique personalities of each team member
- Affirming the contributions of each team member

Communication—"Instead, speaking the truth in love, we will in all things grow up into Him who is the Head, that is, Christ." Ephesians 4:15

Using the way Jesus communicated as our model, Communication means:

- Articulating your ideas in a manner that is clear to the recipient
- Listening intently to one another
- Assuming nothing but clarifying everything
- Sharing the responsibility to understand and be understood

These five concepts define how we will work with one another and what unites us.

> *"There are different kinds of gifts, but the same Spirit. There are different kinds of service, but the same Lord. There are different kinds of working, but the same God works all of them in all persons."*

> 1 Corinthians 12:4–6

APPENDIX 3

The *C.O.S.T.* Team Ministry System[*]

Implementing a biblical model of ministry (Eph. 4) requires an intentional system to assist with application. At Covenant Church, we call our strategy the "*C.O.S.T. Team Ministry System*" (CTMS). Ideally, this developmental and process-oriented system creates a context where life-long servants are encouraged and allowed to be faithful, fruitful, and fulfilled.

Calling

Forming a team...a process to clearly define a ministry's focus and invite called leaders
- *Vision*–articulating a sub-ministry's DNA
- *Identification*–defining the wiring of ministry roles and corresponding names
- *Invitation*–vision casting the contribution for potential servants/disciples/ambassadors

Orienting

Building a team...a process to insure relevant information, training, and team building
- *Information*–providing relevant data for new team members
- *Training*–customized and competency-based skill development
- *Grouping*–team building that allows outsiders to become insiders

Sustaining

Leading a team...a process to keep servants appreciated, growing, and engaged
- *Appreciation*–"putting into" people more than is taken out
- *Development*–coaching investment through relevant leadership styles
- *Empowerment*–apprenticing in order to allow for healthy expansion

Transitioning

Leaving a team...a process to enable servants to exit ministries when appropriate
- *Assessment*–prioritizing a process that provides clear and honest feedback/affirmation
- *Carefrontation*–authentic and gracious communication when servants are not fruitful, fulfilled, and or faithful
- *Referral*–helping servants bridge to their next step of faith

---

[*] © Copyright Network Ministries International. Permission granted via special use permit.

APPENDIX 4

Human Resource Management at Covenant United Methodist Church*

Purpose

To lead, encourage and care for the staff of Covenant United Methodist Church to ensure that each "use[s] whatever gift he has received to serve others" (1 Pet. 4:10) and is able to "prepare God's people for works of service so that the body of Christ may be built up" (Eph. 4:12) in accordance with and in fulfillment of the church's stated mission, vision, values, and beliefs.

Values

Spiritually-Discerning

"Devote yourselves to prayer, being watchful and thankful." COLOSSIANS 4:2

All decisions are to be submitted to God in prayer, grounded in His Word and supplemented by the example of large, Christ-centered churches that prioritize excellence, innovation and a fervent evangelical spirit as their ministry grows.

Mission-Centered

"The body is a unit, though it is made of many parts; and though all its parts are many, they form one body...God has arranged the parts in the body, every one of them, just as He wanted them to be." 1 CORINTHIANS 12:12, 18

First and foremost, individual staff issues, needs, and concerns are always viewed from the perspective of the best interest of the entire staff team and the overall mission of the church (i.e., look at the entire body and how it functions together). Each part is equally as important as another, so all are to be treated with respect and without favoritism.

Gift-Based

"There are different kinds of gifts, but the same Spirit. There are different kinds of service, but the same Lord. There are different kinds of working, but the same God works all of them in all men." 1 CORINTHIANS 12:4–6

---

*This is a reprint of the human resource management policy at Covenant United Methodist Church in Winterville, North Carolina.

Each man has his own gift from God; one has this gift, another has that.
1 CORINTHIANS 12:4–6

"From [Christ] the whole body, joined and held together by every supporting ligament, grows and builds itself up in love, as each part does its work."
EPHESIANS 4:16

The church desires to hire staff that: (1) willingly embrace Covenant's stated mission, vision, values, and beliefs; and (2) have the competency, character, chemistry, and capacity to fulfill the church's mission. Accordingly, the church's managers and lay leadership seek to encourage the longevity of staff by promoting from within whenever possible. Additionally, the church invests in strengthening a staff member's gifts through training and other developmental opportunities that are consistent with its mission. In so doing, the church enables staff to reach their personal development goals as effectively as possible.

Integrity-Driven

"...let us not love with words or tongue, but with actions and in truth."
1 JOHN 3:18

"...speaking the truth in love, we will in all things grow up into him who is the Head, that is Christ." EPHESIANS 4:15

Personnel matters are consistently conducted in an honest and straightforward manner, with an emphasis on active listening. In the process, leaders demonstrate a love for one another not only with words, but with their actions. Accordingly, leaders are accountable to each other, and at all times, confidentiality is honored so that trust is built and maintained.

Balanced

"And what does the LORD require of you? To act justly, love mercy, and to walk humbly with your God" MICAH 6:8

Personnel decisions balance justice and mercy, taking into consideration the needs of the team, any relevant policies, and the staff member's personal needs and circumstances.

Fair

"From the fruit of his lips man is filled with good things, as surely as the work of his hands rewards him" PROVERBS 12:14

The church's compensation system seeks to be both externally competitive and internally consistent, and at all times, seeks to reward diligence, innovation, and excellence.

Consensual

"After this the Lord appointed seventy-two others and sent them two by two ahead of him to every town and place where he was about to go..." LUKE 10:1

Fulfilling the ministry of Christ often—if not always—calls for servants working side by side with others. As a result, personnel decisions at Covenant are typically made by consensus involving appropriate lay and staff leaders as dictated by each situation.

Principles

The following principles are designed to provide general guidelines for how the church's Staff Parish-Pastor Relations Committee (SPPRC) and on-site managers live out the purpose and values outlined above. At the same time, it is understood that there will always be grey areas requiring ongoing communication between various leaders.

In the sections below, the roles of leadership are delineated by two key variables: 1) the stages of human resource management and 2) the classification of employees. The stages are sub-divided into six (6) headings as noted below. Within each, responsibilities are delineated as needed by employment classifications as follows: Full-time equipping staff, full- and part-time ministry coordinators, and support (clerical and facility focused) staff.

Position Creation and Upgrading

All new staff positions and the upgrading of existing ones begin with a detailed proposal including a "Position Description" to the SPPRC. These recommendations are often initiated by staff leaders based on emerging needs within the church. At times, new initiatives are the result of strategic decisions made by the Council in relation to the church's vision. Once consensus among staff and lay leaders is achieved, recommendations are forward to the Finance team for consideration and the Council as needed.

Recruitment and Hiring

The members of the SPPRC are a vital part of the hiring of all full-time equipping staff and the Business Administrator. The process of hiring full- and part-time ministry coordinators is led by the staff in consultation with the Chair of SPPRC. (He or she may choose to be involved or assign another member of SPPRC to participate in the process if so desired.) Support staff is hired by on-site managers and are reported to the SPPRC and its Chair prior to their first day of employment when able.

Daily Operations

On-site managers oversee all daily matters with respect to staff needs, assignments and personnel matters in accordance with the stated values detailed above.

Ministry Planning

On-site managers oversee all matters with respect to ministry planning and related training. The Executive Director keeps the SPPRC up-to-date on critical initiatives and how these are related to the overall direction of the church.

Staff Focus

In concert with the Executive Director, on-site managers provide primary leadership with respect to the scope and focus of a staff member's responsibilities. It is expected that minor changes and adaptations will regularly occur and no need for reporting to the SPPRC is necessary. At other times, staff managers will desire to make changes to Position Descriptions that are significant and involve a transition of job themes or categories. When this is the case with full-time equipping staff and the Business Administrator, it is expected that the SPPRC will be consulted for approval in advance. Delineations between minor and significant job shifts will be made by the Chair of the SPPRC in concert with the Executive Director with the Committee informed as needed.

Discipline and Termination

At all times, the process of discipline and termination detailed in the church's personnel manual is honored. In the case of the support staff and ministry coordinators, these matters are handled by on-site managers and the Chair of the SPPRC is kept informed. He or she then keeps the Committee informed as deemed appropriate. In the case of full-time equipping staff and the Business Administrator, the Chair of SPPRC is kept informed of any discipline matters in progress and informs other Committee members when the employee has received a written warning. Any decision to terminate this level employee is made by the Executive Director and Chair after consultation with the Committee.

Relationships

Communication

The Chair of the SPPRC and the Executive Director are charged with keeping the Committee, the church's leadership and the congregation informed of staff initiatives and their purpose. This is accomplished through a variety of mediums of communication as deemed appropriate in each situation. Additionally, the Executive Director and the Chair of the SPPRC respond as needed to input and feedback from congregational participants.

Executive Director's Relationship with SPPRC

According to the *United Methodist Book of Discipline,* "no staff member...may serve on the committee." Therefore, the Executive Director is expected to attend SPPRC meetings but cannot vote.

Staff in attendance at an SPPRC meeting may be asked to leave the meeting during discussions and decisions of actions that directly involve them. As the leader of the church's staff, the Executive Director reports to the Lead Pastor and is accountable to the SPPRC for the execution of all human resource management matters.

Notes

Foreword

[1]Alexander McCall Smith, *The Full Cupboard of Life* (Pantheon Books, 2003), 126.

[2]William Wordsworth, "The Rainbow" in *The Oxford Book of English Verse 1200-1900,* ed. Arthur Quiller-Couch (Oxford: Clarendon, 1919), found online at www.bartleby.com in April 2006.

Introduction

[1]Lyle Schaller's *Strategies of Change* (Nashville: Abingdon, 1993) helped me to see the value for understanding how to build group consensus for transformation. Leith Anderson's *Dying for Change* (Minneapolis: Bethany House Publishers, 1990) and *A Church for the 21st Century* (Minneapolis: Bethany House Publishers, 1992) showed me how to articulate the need for transformation in light of current cultural trends. Loren Mead's *Transforming Congregations for the Future* (New York: The Alban Institute, 1994) reminded me of the four pillars of a biblical church and how to foster personal transformation through them. Rick Warren's *The Purpose Driven Church* (Grand Rapids: Zondervan, 1995) provided me with a biblically based paradigm for how to balance the multiple purposes of the church and promote structural transformation. Bill Easum's *Sacred Cows Make Gourmet Burgers: Ministry Anytime Anywhere by Anyone* (Nashville: Abingdon, 1995) was particularly helpful to my grasping how to motivate a congregation to first and foremost "give life away" to experience transformation. Tom Bandy's *Kicking Habits: Welcome Relief for Addicted Churches* (Nashville: Abingdon, 1997) and *Moving Off the Map: A Field Guide to Changing the Congregation* (Nashville: Abingdon, 1998) confirmed my own convictions regarding the importance for discerning a clear and God-inspired identity. More recently, Jim Herrington, Mike Bonem, and James H. Furr, *Leading Congregational Change: A Practical Guide for the Transformational Journey* (San Francisco: Jossey-Bass, 2000) and Alan Nelson and Gene Appel, *How to Change Your Church* (Nashville: Word Publishing, 2000) have stimulated my thinking as they insightfully integrate the principles of change management with church life.

[2]Authors such as Peter Senge, John Kotter, Jim Collins, Jerry Porras, Edgar Schein, Richard Beckhard, Everett Rodgers, Rolf Smith, Warren Bennis, Marvin Weisbord, Margaret Wheatley, Harrison Owen, Burt Nanus, and Dee Hock have been most helpful in describing the nature and dynamics of change within human institutions.

[3]Richard J. Foster, *Celebration of Discipline: The Pathway to Spiritual Growth* (San Francisco: Harper and Row, 1978), 6–7.

Chapter 1: Two Kingdoms

[1]George Eldon Ladd, *A Theology of the New Testament* (Grand Rapids: Eerdmans, 1974), 63.

[2]Edgar H. Schein, *The Corporate Culture Survival Guide: Sense and Nonsense About Culture Change* (San Francisco: Jossey-Bass, 1999), 29.

Chapter 2: An Invitation to Exchange

[1]Bill and Lynne Hybels, *Rediscovering Church: The Story and Vision of Willow Creek Community Church* (Grand Rapids: Zondervan, 1995), 67–182.

Chapter 3: An Ongoing Process

[1]Alan C. Klaas, *In Search of the Unchurched* (New York: The Alban Institute, 1996), 103–4.

Chapter 4: A Relative Process

[1]James C. Dobson, *Hide or Seek: Building Self-Esteem in Your Child* (Grand Rapids: Revell, 1974), 23–55.

Chapter 5: A Purposeful Process

[1]Bruce Bugbee, *What You Do Best in the Body of Christ: Discover Your Spiritual Gifts, Personal Style, and God-given Passion* (Grand Rapids: Zondervan, 1995), 52.

[2]For those in the business world, the parallels between a company's human resource function and a church's disciple-making role are striking. When a company is ready to hire someone, its human resources (HR) department starts the ball rolling by *inviting* qualified candidates to apply for the job. During an interview, HR makes sure that the prospects know the company's values, expectations, and needs. Once the right employee is on the job, HR continues its work by *growing* this new company member's contribution through an initial orientation session and an ongoing education, training, and support program. Finally, HR helps with placement—*sending* the new staff member into the area where his or her skills and abilities meet the business' evolving needs. The church and its "invite…grow…send" model is really a HR process designed to help the members *be* and *do.*

[3]Bill Hull, *The Disciple-Making Church* (Grand Rapids: Revell, 1990), 41.

[4]One of my favorite church mission statements that emphasizes these disciple-making themes comes from a dynamic church in Honolulu, The New Hope Christian Fellowship, whose stated purpose is "to introduce people to Jesus Christ, to help them grow to be more like him, and then to reproduce the process in others."

Chapter 6: A Contentious Process

[1]You may—or may not—find comfort knowing that the uncomfortable state of "in between-ness" has been studied and documented. Sociologist Franz Buggle, as reported in the monthly periodical *Religious Watch* (November 2000), conducted research to discover if a link exists between depression and religious beliefs. After 174 interviews, he concluded that those who were highly committed to a belief system—whether religious or atheist—demonstrated the lowest levels of depression. Not surprisingly, the "half" believers and doubters with ties to religion exhibited the highest rates of depression. Perhaps *homelessness* is not just a term to describe those who sleep on the street, but also those whose hearts can't settle on a permanent address, a culture to call their own.

[2]I first ran across this notion of biculturalism in Peter Senge's *The Dance of Change* (New York: Random House, 1999), and it seems more appropriate than the term "bipolar," which is more often associated with internal psychological contention.

Chapter 7: A Cooperative Process

[1]Properly understood, Judaism is also the story of God pursuing man and is the very foundation of Christianity.

[2]For those being introduced to this subject, John Ortberg's *The Life You've Always Wanted* (Grand Rapids: Zondervan, 1997) is an excellent primer. His discussion of the spiritual life marked by *training* versus *trying* is an eye-opener. Spiritual transformation is never about relying on our own efforts and just trying to "be better." Ortberg paints a graphic spiritual picture for us using the metaphor of a person trying to run a marathon without training for it properly (45–48). You can predict the result! Runners who are serious about completing such a race involve every aspect of their lives. They arrange

their hours pounding the pavement and alter their eating and sleeping habits so that all the pieces of their regimen fall into place. Their goal is to be fully trained and ready.

For the more seasoned disciples, I highly recommend the works of Richard Foster and Dallas Willard. Foster's *Celebration of Discipline: The Pathway to Spiritual Growth* (San Francisco: Harper and Row, 1978) has been enormously instrumental in my own growth. He details twelve disciplines that have emerged over the Church's history and subdivides them into three categories: inner, outer and corporate disciplines (see Contents page). Willard's *The Spirit of the Disciplines: Understanding How God Changes Lives* (San Francisco: Harper Collins, 1991) has also helped me understand the partnership of the disciplines and the Spirit's transformational work. His listing is somewhat different than Foster's, but the idea is the same. Willard categorizes the disciplines into two groups: disciplines of abstinence and disciplines of engagement (158). My definition of discipleship—exchanging a world in which we are at the center (putting off or abstaining) for a world in which God is at the center (putting on or engaging)—involves a similar two-step process. Some disciplines are particularly effective at helping me to let go of the world and its values, while other disciplines focus on helping me to embrace God's kingdom.

[3]Richard F. Lovelace, *Dynamics of Spiritual Renewal: An Evangelical Theology of Renewal* (Downers Grove, Ill.: InterVarsity Press, 1979), 75.

[4]Inagrace T. Dietterich, "Missional Community: Cultivating Communities of the Holy Spirit," in *Missional Church: A Vision for the Sending of the Church in North America,* ed. Darrell L. Guder (Grand Rapids: Eerdmans, 1998), 142–82. The author refers to "ecclesial practices" (153) as a means for creating a kingdom culture within the Church, and I have found her writing most helpful.

[5]I am particularly indebted to the thinking of Tom Bandy and Bill Easum with respect to congregational disciplines. Bill's teaching on "leverage points" was a key inspiration to this concept. Tom further reinforces this notion with his writings on church systems in *Christian Chaos: Revolutionizing the Congregation* (Nashville: Abingdon Press, 1999).

Chapter 8: Cornerstone Disciplines

[1]Tom Bandy's book *Moving Off the Map: A Field Guide to Changing the Congregation* (Nashville: Abingdon Press, 1998) and its related workbook are excellent resources for this process. I do, however, disagree with Tom's definition of core values. Rather than understanding the values of a church as those that are currently present, I define these as "the kingdom ideals that Christ is calling a church to embrace as norms of behavior." I believe that a church's values are more helpful if they define the destination, instead of the starting point. By doing so, a vision is cast for where we are to go, much like the spiritual fruit that Paul lays out for us in Galatians 5.

[2]George Bullard, *People of Passion: The Seven Percent,* Spiritual Strategic Journeys Learning Community Series (Hickory, N.C.: Hollifield Leadership Center, 2002).

[3]George Cladis, *The Team-Based Church: How Pastors and Church Staffs Can Grow Together into a Powerful Fellowship of Leaders* (San Francisco: Jossey-Bass, 1999).

[4]First United Methodist Church of Bixby, Oklahoma, has done an excellent job of embedding consensus-building and discernment as a part of its DNA. See http://www.fumcbixby.org/discernment.htm.

[5]Numerous churches provide for this kind of servant development. Two that quickly come to mind are Saddleback's "SALT" (Saddleback's Leadership Training) and Westwinds Community Church's "Frontline" (www.westwinds.org).

Chapter 9: Ministry Disciplines

[1]Mike Puma, "Gable dominated as wrestler and coach," in *Sports Century, Biography, ESPN Classic* Web site, http://espn.go.com/classic/biography/s/Gable_Dan.html.

²Dallas Willard, *Renovation of the Heart: Putting On the Character of Christ* (Colorado Springs: NavPress, 2002), 85.

³David Stark and Patrick Keifert, *Design and Launch a Successful Small Group* (Grand Rapids: Faith Alive Christian Resources, 1994) 6–14.

⁴The most effective team ministry system I have come across is one crafted and taught by Don Cousins along with Bruce Bugbee, and Thomas Nelson will soon be publishing two books that capture their equipping model. The first is Don's book, a theological overview entitled *The Zone of God's Anointing: Leading Your Ministry with God's Presence and Power.* The second is a joint effort of the two entitled *Equipping Leadership.* Also check out www.brucebugbee.com for related training materials and information.

⁵Bruce Bugbee, *What You Do Best in the Body of Christ: Discover Your Spiritual Gifts, Personal Style, and God-given Passion* (Grand Rapids: Zondervan, 1995), 52. These translations are quoted directly from Bugbee's book.

⁶See www.mentorlink.org.

⁷I am particularly impressed with the small group model and accompanying training materials from Church Innovations, which can be reviewed at www.ci.org.

⁸Greg Ogden, *The New Reformation: Returning the Ministry to the People of God* (Grand Rapids: Zondervan, 1990), 85–95.

⁹For those just starting to implement systems to mobilize disciples, I recommend Sue Mallory's resources that can be found at www.connextion.org.

¹⁰Review Bruce Bugbee's passion assessment at www.brucebugbee.com.

¹¹Find out more about Don's coaching and books at www.doncousins.com

Chapter 10: Support Disciplines

¹Eric Bonabeau and Christopher Meyer, "Swarm Intelligence: A Whole New Way to Think About Business," *Harvard Business Review* R0105G (May 2001): 107–14.

²As the church grows into an equipping model of ministry, unpaid equippers will increasingly serve in a managerial role previously dominated by paid staff.

³See www.xpastor.org for insights on this emerging role.

⁴For more information on Crown Ministry, see www.crown.org. Also check out Willow Creek's Good Sense Ministry materials at www.willowcreek.org.

⁵Christian A. Schwartz, *Natural Church Development: A Guide to Eight Essential Qualities of Healthy Churches* (Chicago: Church Smart Resources, 1996) is enjoying growing popularity among leaders of various denominations. Through extensive, worldwide research, Schwartz isolated eight common values among "healthy" churches. Properly understood, these eight essentials are nothing more than the qualitative characteristics of a kingdom church. They are the kingdom ideals we–the Church of Jesus Christ–are being called to embrace as norms of behavior while at the same time being called to let go of the antithetical values of the world. As you can see, we have come to the same conclusions through different paths.

Bibliography

Anderson, Leith. *Dying for Change*. Minneapolis: Bethany House, 1990.

_____. *A Church for the 21ˢᵗ Century*. Minneapolis: Bethany House, 1992.

Anderson, Neil T., and Charles Mylander. *Setting Your Church Free*. Ventura: Regal Books, 1994.

Bandy, Thomas G. *Christian Chaos: Revolutionizing the Congregation*. Nashville: Abingdon Press, 1999.

_____. *Kicking Habits: Welcome Relief for Addicted Churches*. Nashville: Abingdon Press, 1997.

_____. *Moving Off the Map: A Field Guide to Changing the Congregation*. Nashville: Abingdon Press, 1998.

Bonabeau, Eric, and Christopher Meyer. "Swarm Intelligence: A Whole New Way to Think About Business." Reprint R0105G. *Harvard Business Review*. Cambridge: Harvard Business School, 2001.

Bridges, William. *Managing Transitions: Making the Most of Change*. Reading, Mass.: Perseus Books, 1991.

Bugbee, Bruce. *What You Do Best in the Body of Christ: Discover Your Spiritual Gifts, Personal Style, and God-given Passion*. Grand Rapids: Zondervan, 1995.

Bullard, George. *People of Passion: The Seven Percent*. Hickory, N.C.: Hollifield, 2002.

Cladis, George. *The Team-Based Church: How Pastors and Church Staffs Can Grow Together into a Powerful Fellowship of Leaders*. San Francisco: Jossey-Bass, 1999.

Dietterich, Inagrace T. "Missional Community: Cultivating Communities of the Holy Spirit." In *Missional Church: A Vision for the Sending of the Church in North America*. Edited by Darrell L. Guder, 142–82. Grand Rapids: Eerdmans, 1998.

Dobson, James C. *Hide or Seek: Building Self-Esteem in Your Child*. Grand Rapids: Revell, 1974.

Easum, William M. *Sacred Cows Make Gourmet Burgers: Ministry Anytime Anywhere by Anyone*. Nashville: Abingdon Press, 1995.

Easum, William M., and Thomas G. Bandy. *Growing Spiritual Redwoods*. Nashville: Abingdon Press, 1997.

Foster, Richard J. *Celebration of Discipline: The Pathway to Spiritual Growth*. San Francisco: Harper and Row, 1978.

Herrington, Jim, Mike Bonem, and James H. Furr. *Leading Congregational Change: A Practical Guide for the Transformational Journey.* San Francisco: Jossey-Bass, 2000.

Hull, Bill. *The Disciple-Making Church.* Grand Rapids: Revell, 1990.

Hybels, Bill, and Lynne Hybels. *Rediscovering Church: The Story and Vision of Willow Creek Community Church.* Grand Rapids: Zondervan, 1995.

Jordan, Clarence. *Sermon on the Mount.* Valley Forge: Judson Press, 1952.

Klaas, Alan C. *In Search of the Unchurched.* New York: The Alban Institute, 1996.

Ladd, George Eldon. *A Commentary on Revelation.* Grand Rapids: Eerdmans, 1972.

_____. *Crucial Questions about the Kingdom of God.* Grand Rapids: Eerdmans,

_____. *A Theology of the New Testament.* Grand Rapids: Eerdmans, 1974.

1952.

Lovelace, Richard F. *Dynamics of Spiritual Renewal: An Evangelical Theology of Renewal.* Downers Grove, Ill.: InterVarsity Press, 1979.

Mead, Loren B. *Transforming Congregations for the Future.* New York: The Alban Institute, 1994.

Nelson, Alan, and Gene Appel. *How to Change Your Church Without Killing It.* Nashville: Word Publishing, 2000.

Ogden, Greg. *The New Reformation: Returning the Ministry to the People of God.* Grand Rapids: Zondervan, 1992.

Ortberg, John. *The Life You've Always Wanted.* Grand Rapids: Zondervan, 1997.

Puma, Mike. "Gable dominated as wrestler and coach." *Sports Century Biography, ESPN Classic* Web site, http://espn.go.com/classic/biography/s/Gable_Dan.html.

Schaller, Lyle E. *Strategies for Change.* Nashville: Abingdon Press, 1993.

Schein, Edgar H. *The Corporate Culture Survival Guide: Sense and Nonsense About Culture Change.* San Francisco: Jossey-Bass, 1999.

Stark, David, and Patrick Keifert. *Design and Launch a Successful Small Group.* Grand Rapids: Faith Alive Christian Resources, 1994.

Schwartz, Christian A. *Natural Church Development: A Guide to Eight Essential Qualities of Healthy Churches.* Chicago: Church Smart Resources, 1996.

Tuttle, Robert G., Jr. *Can We Talk: Sharing Your Faith in a Pre-Christian World.* Nashville: Abingdon Press, 1999.

_____. *Sanctity Without Starch: A Layperson's Guide to a Wesleyan Theology of Grace.* Lexington: Bristol Books, 1992.

Warren, Rick. *The Purpose Driven Church.* Grand Rapids: Zondervan, 1995.

Wilkins, Michael J. *Following the Master: A Biblical Theology of Discipleship.* Grand Rapids: Zondervan, 1992.

Willard, Dallas. *Renovation of the Heart: Putting on the Character of Christ.* Colorado Springs: NavPress, 2002.

_____. *The Spirit of the Disciplines: Understanding How God Changes Lives.* San Francisco: Harper Collins, 1991.

Online Sources

www.brucebugbee.com
www.ci.org
www.connextion.org
www.crown.org
www.doncoursins.com
http://www.fumcbixby.org/discernment/htm
www.mentorlink.org
www.westwinds.org
www.xpastor.org